KITCHEN LIBRARY
Mains

KITCHEN LIBRARY
Mains

MURDOCH BOOKS

contents

Classic and Contemporary Favourites

When it comes to cooking a main course, there are limitless possibilities. What you choose depends on a few considerations, such as the occasion, the season and also a guest's dietary needs. Often the decision of what to cook is complicated by cookbooks themselves – few are actually devoted exclusively to the main course and the cook must consult a range of books to find just the right recipe. *Kitchen Library Mains* brings together the entire spectrum of main course dishes, making choosing painless. From laid-back family meals to the swishest of offerings, all the favourites are here.

There's endless inspiration for entertaining. Seafood, for example, suggests luxury, whether in the form of seared scallops, a whole baked fish or a complex stew such as bouillabaisse. Refined meat dishes, such as rabbit with rosemary and red wine, or herbed rack of veal, will similarly satisfy the most discerning of palates and look impressive, too. When the occasion calls for a more casual approach, there are dozens of ideas. Barbecued food is the quintessential relaxed fare and, when fine weather allows for outdoor dining, there is nothing more delicious than the aroma of skewers, steaks or cutlets as they sizzle over an open flame.

Beyond entertaining and special occasions, there's the inescapable routine of providing family meals – without fresh ideas, cooking every night can become a chore. From classic to contemporary, from fast to fussy, and from the very familiar to the exoticism of foreign cuisines, the recipes in *Kitchen Library Mains* will supply a recipe for any occasion.

seafood

Seafood, Fennel and Potato Stew

※ SERVES 6
※ PREPARATION TIME: 25 MINUTES
※ COOKING TIME: 30 MINUTES

18–20 black mussels
6 baby octopus
16 raw prawns (shrimp)
1 large fennel bulb
2 tablespoons olive oil
2 leeks, white part only, thinly sliced
2 garlic cloves, crushed
$1/2$ teaspoon paprika
2 tablespoons Pernod or Ricard (see Notes)
170 ml ($5^1/2$ fl oz/$^2/_3$ cup) dry white wine
$1/4$ teaspoon saffron threads
$1/4$ teaspoon thyme
500 g (1 lb 2 oz) fish cutlets (such as
    swordfish, mulloway, warehou), cut
    into 6 large chunks
400 g (14 oz) small boiling potatoes
    (see Notes)

Scrub the mussels with a stiff brush and pull out the hairy beards. Discard any broken mussels or open ones that don't close when tapped on the bench. Rinse well.

Use a small, sharp knife to cut off the octopus heads. Grasp the bodies and push the beaks out with your index finger. Remove and discard. Slit the heads and remove the gut, then wash well.

Peel the prawns, leaving the tails intact. Gently pull out the dark vein from each prawn back, starting at the head end.

Remove the fennel fronds and reserve. Trim off any discoloured parts of the fennel and thinly slice. Heat the oil in a large frying pan over medium heat. Add the fennel, leek and garlic. Stir in the paprika, season lightly and cook for 8 minutes, or until softened. Add the Pernod or Ricard and wine and boil for 1 minute, or until reduced by one-third.

Add the mussels to the pan, cover and cook, shaking the pan occasionally for 4–5 minutes, discarding any mussels that haven't opened after that time. Remove from the pan and allow to cool. Remove the mussel meat from the shells and set aside.

Add the saffron and thyme to the pan and cook, stirring over medium heat, for 1–2 minutes. Season if necessary, then transfer to a large, flameproof casserole dish.

Stir the octopus, prawns, fish and potatoes into the stew. Cover and cook gently for 10 minutes, or until the potatoes and seafood are tender. Add the mussels, cover and heat through. Garnish with the reserved fennel fronds and serve.

NOTES: Pernod and Ricard are aniseed-flavoured liqueurs that complement the fennel.
   Choose very small potatoes for this recipe. Otherwise, cut larger ones in half. Waxy potatoes will produce the best result.

John Dory with Prawns and Creamy Dill Sauce

✿ SERVES 4
✿ PREPARATION TIME: 15 MINUTES
✿ COOKING TIME: 20 MINUTES

12 raw large prawns (shrimp)
625 ml (21½ fl oz/2½ cups) fish stock
30 g (1 oz) butter
1 garlic clove, finely chopped
2 tablespoons plain (all-purpose) flour
2 tablespoons cream
olive oil, for pan-frying
4 x 200 g (7 oz) john dory fillets
1 tablespoon snipped chives
1 tablespoon chopped dill
chives or dill sprigs, to garnish

Peel the prawns, leaving the tails intact. Gently pull out the dark vein from each prawn back, starting from the head end. Heat the stock in a saucepan and bring to the boil. Reduce the heat and simmer for 10 minutes, or until the liquid has reduced. You will need 375 ml (13 fl oz/1½ cups) fish stock.

Melt the butter in a small saucepan and add the garlic. Stir in the flour and cook for 1 minute, or until pale and foaming. Remove from the heat and gradually stir in the stock. Return to the heat and stir constantly until the sauce boils and thickens. Reduce the heat and simmer for 1 minute. Remove from the heat and stir in the cream. Season to taste. Keep warm.

Heat a little oil in a frying pan and cook the fish fillets over medium heat for 2 minutes each side, or until the fish flakes easily when tested with a fork. Transfer to serving plates. Add the prawns to the same pan and cook for 2–3 minutes. Stir the chives and dill into the sauce, arrange the prawns and spoon the sauce over the top. Garnish with chives or dill.

Tuna with Sorrel Hollandaise

✿ SERVES 4
✿ PREPARATION TIME: 15 MINUTES
✿ COOKING TIME: 10 MINUTES

SORREL HOLLANDAISE
15 young sorrel leaves, stems removed
150 g (5½ oz) butter
3 egg yolks
1 tablespoon lemon juice

4 x 150 g (5½ oz) tuna steaks
2 tablespoons olive oil

To make the sorrel hollandaise, put the sorrel leaves in a bowl, cover with boiling water, drain and rinse in cold water. Pat the leaves dry with paper towels and chop roughly. Melt the butter in a small saucepan. Put the egg yolks in a food processor and process for 20 seconds. With the motor running, add the hot butter in a thin, steady stream and process until thick and creamy. Add the lemon juice and sorrel and season to taste. Process for another 20 seconds.

Brush the tuna with the oil. Heat a large frying pan and cook the tuna for 2–3 minutes each side over medium heat. Spoon the sorrel hollandaise over the tuna and serve.

John Dory with Prawns and Creamy Dill Sauce

Caponata with Tuna

❀ SERVES 6
❀ PREPARATION TIME: 25 MINUTES
❀ COOKING TIME: 45 MINUTES

CAPONATA
750 g (1 lb 10 oz) eggplant (aubergine),
    cut into 1 cm (½ inch) cubes
125 ml (4 fl oz/½ cup) olive oil
1 onion, chopped
3 celery stalks, chopped
500 g (1 lb 2 oz) ripe tomatoes, peeled
    and cut into 1 cm (½ inch) cubes
2 tablespoons capers, rinsed and squeezed
    dry
115 g (4 oz/⅔ cup) green olives, pitted
1 tablespoon sugar
125 ml (4 fl oz/½ cup) red wine vinegar

6 x 200 g (7 oz) tuna steaks
olive oil, for brushing

Sprinkle the eggplant with salt and leave in a colander for 1 hour. Rinse under cold water and pat dry. Heat 2 tablespoons of the oil in a frying pan over medium heat and cook half the eggplant for 4–5 minutes, or until golden and soft. Remove from the pan and drain on crumpled paper towels. Repeat with another 2 tablespoons of the oil and the remaining eggplant.

Heat the remaining olive oil in the same pan, add the onion and celery, and cook for 5–6 minutes, or until softened. Reduce the heat to low, add the tomato and simmer for 15 minutes. Stir in the capers, olives, sugar and vinegar, season and continue to simmer for 10 minutes, or until slightly reduced. Stir in the eggplant. Remove from the heat and cool.

Heat a chargrill plate and brush lightly with olive oil. Cook the tuna for 2–3 minutes each side, or to your liking. Serve with the caponata.

Pan-Fried Salmon with Gremolata

❀ SERVES 4
❀ PREPARATION TIME: 10 MINUTES
❀ COOKING TIME: 10 MINUTES

GREMOLATA
4 tablespoons finely chopped flat-leaf
    (Italian) parsley
2 teaspoons grated lemon zest
2 teaspoons grated orange zest
2 garlic cloves, crushed
3 teaspoons capers, rinsed and
    squeezed dry

30 g (1 oz) butter
1 tablespoon olive oil
4 x 200 g (7 oz) salmon fillets

To make the gremolata, combine the parsley, lemon and orange zest and garlic in a small bowl with the capers. Mix well and set aside.

Heat a large frying pan and add the butter and olive oil. Add the salmon fillets and pan-fry over high heat on both sides for about 2–3 minutes each side, or until cooked as desired. Serve topped with the gremolata.

Caponata with Tuna

Baked Fish with Noodle Filling

* SERVES 10–12
* PREPARATION TIME: 20 MINUTES
* COOKING TIME: 50 MINUTES

2 kg (4 lb 8 oz) ocean trout or 1 whole
   salmon, boned and butterflied
   (see Note)
100 g (3½ oz) rice stick noodles
1 tablespoon peanut oil
6 red Asian shallots or French shallots,
   chopped
2 red chillies, chopped
2 tablespoons grated fresh ginger
200 g (7 oz) water chestnuts, chopped
200 g (7 oz) bamboo shoots, chopped
6 spring onions (scallions), sliced
2 tablespoons chopped coriander (cilantro)
   root
3 tablespoons chopped coriander (cilantro)
   leaves
2 tablespoons fish sauce
2 tablespoons grated palm sugar (jaggery)
   or soft brown sugar

LIME BUTTER SAUCE
4 kaffir lime leaves, finely shredded
2 tablespoons lime juice
125 g (4½ oz) butter

Preheat the oven to 180°C (350°F/Gas 4). Pat the fish dry and use tweezers to remove any remaining small bones.

Soak the noodles in boiling water for 10 minutes. Drain well, pat dry and cut into short lengths.

Heat the oil in a frying pan and cook the shallots, chilli and ginger over medium heat for about 5 minutes, or until the shallots are golden. Transfer to a bowl. Add the noodles, water chestnuts, bamboo shoots, spring onion, coriander root and leaves, fish sauce and palm sugar to the bowl and mix well.

Open the trout or salmon out flat and spread the noodle filling over the centre. Fold the fish over to enclose the filling and secure with string every 5 cm (2 inches) along the fish. Place onto a baking tray lined with foil and bake for 30–40 minutes, or until tender.

To make the sauce, put the kaffir lime leaves, lime juice and butter in a saucepan and cook over medium heat until the butter turns nutty brown.

Cut the salmon into slices, discarding the string, then serve topped with the sauce.

NOTE: A fish that has been butterflied has been carefully slit through the middle, along the bones, but not all the way through. The effect is of having a hinge on one side of the fish. Another term for this is 'pocket boning'. Ask your fishmonger to do this for you.

Steamed Fish Cutlets with Ginger and Chilli

❧ SERVES 4
❧ PREPARATION TIME: 15 MINUTES
❧ COOKING TIME: 10 MINUTES

4 x 200 g (7 oz) skinless firm white
    fish cutlets
5 cm (2 inch) piece fresh ginger, cut into
    fine shreds
2 garlic cloves, chopped
2 teaspoons chopped red chilli
2 tablespoons finely chopped coriander
    (cilantro) stems
3 spring onions (scallions), cut into fine
    shreds each 4 cm (1½ inches) long
2 tablespoons lime juice
lime wedges, to serve

Line a bamboo steaming basket with banana leaves or baking paper (this is so the fish will not stick or taste of bamboo).

Arrange the fish cutlets in the basket and top with the ginger, garlic, chilli and coriander. Cover and steam over a wok or large saucepan of boiling water for 5–6 minutes.

Remove the lid and sprinkle the spring onion and lime juice over the fish. Cover and steam for 30 seconds, or until the fish is cooked. Serve immediately with wedges of lime and steamed rice.

Grilled Fish with Fennel and Lemon

❧ SERVES 4
❧ PREPARATION TIME: 10 MINUTES
❧ COOKING TIME: 10 MINUTES

4 whole red mullet or bream, cleaned,
    scaled and gutted
1 lemon, thinly sliced
1 baby fennel bulb, thinly sliced
1½ tablespoons fennel seeds
60 ml (2 fl oz/¼ cup) lemon juice
80 ml (2½ fl oz/⅓ cup) olive oil

Cut three diagonal slashes on both sides of each fish. Put two or three slices of lemon and some slices of fennel bulb in the cavity of each fish. Bruise the fennel seeds roughly, using a mortar and pestle. Sprinkle both sides of each fish with the cracked fennel seeds and some salt and rub well into the flesh.

Mix the lemon juice and olive oil in a bowl. Heat a chargrill pan or plate and when very hot, add the fish. Drizzle a little of the juice and oil over each fish. After 5 minutes, turn carefully with tongs, ensuring the filling doesn't fall out, and drizzle with the oil mixture. Gently flake a piece of flesh with a fork to test whether it is cooked through, then serve with salad.

Steamed Fish Cutlets with Ginger and Chilli

Zarzuela

❧ SERVES 4
❧ PREPARATION TIME: 40 MINUTES
❧ COOKING TIME: 1 HOUR 10 MINUTES

SOFRITO SAUCE

1 tablespoon olive oil
2 onions, finely chopped
2 large tomatoes, peeled, seeded and
    roughly chopped
1 tablespoon tomato paste (concentrated
    purée)

PICADA SAUCE

3 slices white bread, crusts removed
1 tablespoon almonds, toasted
3 garlic cloves
1 tablespoon olive oil

1 raw lobster tail (about 400 g/14 oz)
12–15 black mussels
750 g (1 lb 10 oz) skinless firm white fish
    fillets, cut into bite-sized pieces
plain (all-purpose) flour, seasoned
2–3 tablespoons olive oil
125 g (4½ oz) calamari rings
12 large raw prawns (shrimp)
125 ml (4 fl oz/½ cup) white wine
125 ml (4 fl oz/½ cup) brandy
3 tablespoons chopped flat-leaf (Italian)
    parsley, to garnish

To make the sofrito sauce, heat the oil in a saucepan over medium heat. Add the onion and stir for 5 minutes without browning. Add the tomato, tomato paste and 125 ml (4 fl oz/½ cup) water and stir over medium heat for 10 minutes. Stir in another 125 ml (4 fl oz/½ cup) water, season and set aside.

To make the picada sauce, finely chop the bread, almonds and garlic in a food processor. With the motor running, gradually add the oil to form a paste, adding another ½ tablespoon of oil if necessary.

Preheat the oven to 180°C (350°F/Gas 4). Cut the lobster tail into rounds through the membrane that separates the shell segments. Set the rounds aside. Scrub the mussels with a stiff brush and pull out the hairy beards. Discard any broken mussels, or open ones that don't close when tapped on the bench. Rinse well.

Lightly coat the fish in the flour. Heat the oil in a large frying pan and fry the fish in batches over medium heat for 2–3 minutes, or until cooked and golden brown all over. Transfer to a large casserole dish. Add a little oil to the pan if necessary, add the calamari and cook, stirring, for 1–2 minutes. Remove and add to the fish. Cook the lobster rounds and prawns for 2–3 minutes, or until the prawns turn pink, then add to the soup.

Add the wine to the pan and bring to the boil. Reduce the heat, add the mussels, cover and steam for 4–5 minutes. Add to the soup, discarding any unopened mussels. Ensuring nothing flammable is nearby, pour the brandy into one side of the pan. When it has warmed, carefully ignite the brandy. Gently shake the pan until the flames have died down. Pour this mixture over the seafood in the casserole dish. Pour the sofrito sauce over the top. Cover and bake for 20 minutes. Stir in the picada sauce and cook for a further 10 minutes, or until warmed through – do not overcook or the seafood will toughen. Sprinkle with parsley and serve.

Baked Fish with Tomato and Onion

❧ SERVES 4

❧ PREPARATION TIME: 20 MINUTES

❧ COOKING TIME: 45 MINUTES

60 ml (2 fl oz/¼ cup) olive oil

2 onions, finely chopped

1 small celery stalk, finely chopped

1 small carrot, finely chopped

2 garlic cloves, chopped

400 g (14 oz) tinned chopped tomatoes

2 tablespoons tomato passata (puréed
  tomatoes)

¼ teaspoon dried oregano

½ teaspoon sugar

50 g (1¾ oz) stale white bread

500 g (1 lb 2 oz) skinless firm white fish
  fillets

3 tablespoons chopped flat-leaf (Italian)
  parsley

1 tablespoon lemon juice

Preheat the oven to 180°C (350°F/Gas 4). Heat 2 tablespoons of the oil in a heavy-based frying pan. Add the onion, celery and carrot and cook over low heat for 10 minutes, or until soft. Add the garlic, cook for 2 minutes, then add the chopped tomatoes, tomato passata, oregano and sugar. Simmer for 10 minutes, stirring occasionally, until reduced and thickened. Season to taste.

To make the breadcrumbs, chop the bread in a food processor for a few minutes, until fine crumbs form.

Arrange the fish in a single layer in an ovenproof dish. Stir the parsley and lemon juice into the sauce. Season to taste, and pour over the fish. Scatter the breadcrumbs all over the top and drizzle with the remaining oil. Bake for 20 minutes, or until the fish is just cooked.

Fish Fillets with Harissa and Olives

❧ SERVES 4

❧ PREPARATION TIME: 15 MINUTES

❧ COOKING TIME: 25 MINUTES

80 ml (2½ fl oz/⅓ cup) olive oil

4 skinless firm white fish fillets

seasoned flour, for dusting

1 onion, chopped

2 garlic cloves, crushed

400 g (14 oz) tinned chopped tomatoes

2 teaspoons harissa

2 bay leaves

1 cinnamon stick

185 g (6½ oz/1 cup) kalamata olives

1 tablespoon lemon juice

2 tablespoons chopped flat-leaf (Italian)
  parsley

Heat half the olive oil in a heavy-based frying pan. Dust the fish fillets with flour and cook over medium heat for 2 minutes each side, or until golden. Transfer to a plate.

Add the remaining olive oil to the pan and cook the onion and garlic for 3–4 minutes, or until softened. Add the chopped tomatoes, harissa, bay leaves and cinnamon. Cook for 10 minutes, or until the sauce has thickened. Season to taste.

Return the fish to the pan, add the olives and cover the fish with the sauce. Remove the bay leaves and cinnamon stick and continue cooking for 2 minutes, or until the fish is tender. Add the lemon juice and parsley and serve.

Baked Fish with Tomato and Onion

Stuffed Squid with Rice

8 small squid
about 2 teaspoons plain (all-purpose) flour

STUFFING
1 small onion
2 tablespoons olive oil
2 tablespoons currants
2 tablespoons pine nuts
25 g (1 oz/1/3 cup) fresh breadcrumbs
1 tablespoon chopped mint
1 tablespoon chopped flat-leaf (Italian)
    parsley
1 egg, lightly beaten

SAUCE
1 tablespoon olive oil
1 small onion, finely chopped
1 garlic clove, crushed
60 ml (2 fl oz/1/4 cup) dry white wine
400 g (14 oz) tinned chopped tomatoes
1/2 teaspoon sugar
1 bay leaf

RICE
1.25 litres (44 fl oz/5 cups) fish stock
60 ml (2 fl oz/1/4 cup) olive oil
1 onion, finely chopped
3 garlic cloves, crushed
275 g (9 3/4 oz/1 1/4 cups) calasparra or
    short-grain white rice
1/4 teaspoon cayenne pepper
3 teaspoons squid ink or four 4 g sachets
60 ml (2 fl oz/1/4 cup) dry white wine
60 g (2 1/4 oz/1/4 cup) tomato paste
    (concentrated purée)
2 tablespoons chopped flat-leaf (Italian)
    parsley

To clean the squid, pull each body from the tentacles. Cut off and keep the tentacles as well as the fins from either side of each body sac. If using the ink sacs, extract them and squeeze the ink into a small bowl. Peel the skin from each body sac and dislodge and remove the quills. Rinse under cold water.

To make the stuffing, in a food processor, finely chop the tentacles, fins and onion. Heat the oil in a frying pan and cook the currants and pine nuts over low heat, stirring until the nuts are lightly browned. Transfer to a bowl using a slotted spoon. Add the onion mixture to the pan and cook gently over low heat for 5 minutes. Add to the bowl and add the breadcrumbs, mint, parsley and egg. Season and mix well. Stuff into the squid bodies. Close the openings and secure with toothpicks. Dust the squid with the flour.

To make the sauce, wipe out the frying pan with paper towels. Heat the oil, add the onion and cook over low heat for 5 minutes, or until softened. Stir in the garlic, cook for 30 seconds, then add the wine. Cook over high heat for 1 minute, then add the tomato, sugar and bay leaf. Season, reduce the heat and simmer for 5 minutes. Stir in 125 ml (4 fl oz/1/2 cup) water. Place the squid in the pan in a single layer. Simmer, covered, for about 20 minutes, or until the squid are tender.

To make the rice, bring the stock to a simmer in a saucepan. Heat the oil in a large saucepan, add the onion and cook over low heat for 5 minutes, or until softened. Add the garlic, cook for 15 seconds, then stir in the rice and cayenne pepper. Mix the ink with 80 ml (2 1/2 fl oz/1/3 cup) of hot stock. Stir into the rice, then add the wine and tomato paste. Stir until the liquid has almost all evaporated, then add 250 ml (9 fl oz/1 cup) of the hot stock. Simmer until this evaporates, then stir in more stock, 250 ml (9 fl oz/1 cup) at a time, until the rice is tender and creamy, about 15 minutes. Cover the pan and leave off the heat for 5 minutes. Season well.

To serve, spread the rice on a warm platter and stir in the parsley. Arrange the squid on top and spoon on the sauce.

Seafood Paella

❧ SERVES 6

❧ PREPARATION TIME: 25 MINUTES

❧ COOKING TIME: 45 MINUTES

500 g (1 lb 2 oz) raw prawns (shrimp)

250 g (9 oz) black mussels

200 g (7 oz) squid rings

60 ml (2 fl oz/¼ cup) olive oil

1 large onion, diced

3 garlic cloves, finely chopped

1 small red capsicum (pepper), seeded
    and membrane removed, thinly sliced

1 small red chilli, seeded and chopped
    (optional)

2 teaspoons paprika

1 teaspoon ground turmeric

2 tomatoes, peeled, seeded and finely
    chopped

1 tablespoon tomato paste (concentrated
    purée)

440 g (15½ oz/2 cups) paella rice or
    risotto rice

125 ml (4 fl oz/½ cup) dry white wine

¼ teaspoon saffron threads, soaked in
    60 ml (2 fl oz/¼ cup) hot water

1.25 litres (44 fl oz/5 cups) fish stock

300 g (10½ oz) skinless firm white fish
    fillets, cut into 2.5 cm (1 inch) cubes

3 tablespoons chopped flat-leaf (Italian)
    parsley, to serve

lemon wedges, to serve

Peel the prawns, leaving the tails intact. Gently pull out the dark vein from each prawn back, starting at the head end. Scrub the mussels with a stiff brush and pull out the hairy beards. Discard any broken mussels or open ones that don't close when tapped on the bench. Rinse well. Cover the seafood (including the squid) and refrigerate, until ready to use.

Heat the oil in a paella pan or large, deep frying pan with a lid. Add the onion, garlic, capsicum and chilli and cook over medium heat for 2 minutes, or until the onion and capsicum are soft. Add the paprika, turmeric and 1 teaspoon salt and stir-fry for 1–2 minutes, or until fragrant.

Add the chopped tomatoes and cook for 5 minutes, or until softened. Add the tomato paste and stir in the rice until it is well coated.

Pour in the wine and simmer until almost absorbed. Add the saffron and its soaking liquid and all the fish stock and bring to the boil. Reduce the heat and simmer for 20 minutes, or until almost all the liquid is absorbed into the rice. There is no need to stir the rice, but you may occasionally wish to fluff it up with a fork to separate the grains.

Add the mussels to the pan, poking the shells into the rice, cover and cook for 1–2 minutes over low heat. Add the prawns and cook for 2–3 minutes. Add the fish, cover and cook for 3 minutes. Finally, add the squid rings and cook for 1–2 minutes. By this time, the mussels should have opened – discard any unopened ones. The prawns should be pink and the fish should flake easily when tested with a fork. The squid should be white, moist and tender. Cook for another 2–3 minutes if the seafood is not quite cooked, but avoid overcooking or the seafood will toughen and dry out. Remove the pan from the heat, cover loosely with foil and leave to rest for 5–10 minutes. Serve with the parsley and lemon wedges. Delicious with a tossed salad.

Chu Chee Seafood Curry

⁂ SERVES 4
⁂ PREPARATION TIME: 20 MINUTES
⁂ COOKING TIME: 20 MINUTES

500 g (1 lb 2 oz) raw king prawns
    (shrimp)
500 g (1 lb 2 oz) scallops, without roe
2 x 270 ml (9½ fl oz) tins coconut cream
    (do not shake)
55 g (2 oz/¼ cup) chu chee curry paste
    (see Note)
2–3 tablespoons fish sauce
2–3 tablespoons grated palm sugar
    (jaggery) or soft brown sugar
8 kaffir lime leaves, finely shredded
2 small red chillies, thinly sliced (optional)
1 very large handful Thai basil

Peel the prawns, leaving the tails intact. Gently pull out the dark vein from each prawn back, starting at the head end. Remove and discard any veins, membrane or hard white muscle from the scallops.

Lift off the thick cream from the top of the coconut cream — there should be about 250 ml (9 fl oz/1 cup) of cream — and put it in a wok. Bring to the boil, then stir in the curry paste. Reduce the heat and simmer for 10 minutes, or until fragrant and the oil begins to separate from the cream.

Stir in the seafood and remaining coconut cream and cook for 5 minutes. Add the fish sauce, palm sugar, kaffir lime leaves and chilli and cook for 1 minute. Stir in half the basil and use the rest to garnish.

NOTE: Chu chee curry paste can be bought from Asian food speciality stores.

Fish Rolls

❀ SERVES 4

❀ PREPARATION TIME: 25 MINUTES

❀ COOKING TIME: 20 MINUTES

1 large ripe tomato, peeled, seeded and
    roughly chopped
1 tablespoon drained capers, chopped
40 g (1½ oz) stuffed green olives, chopped
3 tablespoons chopped lemon thyme
30 g (1 oz) romano cheese, finely grated
2 teaspoons finely grated lemon zest
8 thin firm skinless white fish fillets (such
    as john dory, bream, perch, snapper)
250 ml (9 fl oz/1 cup) dry white wine
2 tablespoons lemon juice
3 tablespoons lemon thyme
2 bay leaves

Preheat the oven to 160°C (315°F/Gas 2–3). Put the tomato in a small bowl and mix with the capers, olives, thyme, cheese, lemon zest and ¼ teaspoon freshly ground black pepper.

Place the fillets, skinned side up, on a flat surface. Spread the tomato mixture evenly onto each fillet, then roll tightly and secure with a toothpick or skewer. Place in a single layer in a shallow casserole dish.

Pour the combined wine, lemon juice, thyme and bay leaves over the fish, cover and bake for 20 minutes, or until the fish is cooked and flakes easily when tested with a fork.

Barbecued Seafood Platter

❋ SERVES 6
❋ PREPARATION TIME: 40 MINUTES
❋ COOKING TIME: 30 MINUTES

6 Balmain bugs
30 g (1 oz) butter, melted
1 tablespoon oil
12 black mussels
12 scallops, on the shell
12 oysters
18 raw large prawns (shrimp), unpeeled

SALSA VERDE
1 tablespoon chopped preserved lemon
20 g (³⁄₄ oz/²⁄₃ cup) flat-leaf (Italian)
   parsley
1 tablespoon drained capers
1 tablespoon lemon juice
3 tablespoons olive oil

VINEGAR AND SHALLOT DRESSING
60 ml (2 fl oz/¹⁄₄ cup) white wine vinegar
4 French shallots, finely chopped
1 tablespoon chopped chervil

PICKLED GINGER AND WASABI SAUCE
1 teaspoon soy sauce
60 ml (2 fl oz/¹⁄₄ cup) mirin
2 tablespoons rice wine vinegar
¹⁄₄ teaspoon wasabi paste
2 tablespoons finely sliced pickled ginger

SWEET BALSAMIC DRESSING
1 tablespoon olive oil
1 tablespoon honey
125 ml (4 fl oz/¹⁄₂ cup) balsamic vinegar

THAI CORIANDER SAUCE
125 ml (4 fl oz/¹⁄₂ cup) sweet chilli sauce
1 tablespoon lime juice
2 tablespoons chopped coriander (cilantro)

Freeze the bugs or lobsters for 1 hour to immobilise. Cut each bug in half with a sharp knife, then brush the flesh with the combined butter and oil. Set aside.

Scrub the mussels with a stiff brush and pull out the hairy beards. Discard any broken mussels, or open ones that don't close when tapped on the bench. Rinse well.

Pull off any vein, membrane or hard white muscle from the scallops, leaving any roe attached. Brush the scallops with the combined butter and oil. Cook them, shell side down, on the barbecue.

Remove the oysters from the shells, then rinse the shells under cold water. Pat the shells dry and return the oysters to their shells. Cover and refrigerate all the seafood while you make the dressings.

To make the salsa verde, combine all the ingredients in a food processor and process in short bursts until chopped. Transfer to a bowl and add enough oil to moisten the mixture. Season. Serve a dollop on each scallop.

To make the vinegar and shallot dressing, whisk the vinegar, shallot and chervil in a bowl until combined. Pour over the cooked mussels.

To make the pickled ginger and wasabi sauce, whisk all the ingredients in a bowl until combined. Spoon over the cooked oysters.

To make the sweet balsamic dressing, heat the oil in a pan, add the honey and vinegar, bring to the boil, then boil until reduced by half. Drizzle over the cooked bugs.

To make the Thai coriander sauce, combine all the ingredients in a jug and drizzle over the cooked prawns.

Cook the seafood on a preheated barbecue hotplate. The mussels, scallops, oysters and prawns all take about 2–5 minutes to cook. The bugs are cooked when the flesh turns white and starts to come away from the shell.

Seafood Lasagne

* SERVES 4–6
* PREPARATION TIME: 15 MINUTES
* COOKING TIME: 45 MINUTES

250 g (9 oz) instant lasagne sheets
125 g (4½ oz) scallops
500 g (1 lb 2 oz) raw prawns (shrimp)
500 g (1 lb 2 oz) skinless firm white fish fillets (such as hake, snapper, gemfish or ling)
125 g (4½ oz) butter
1 leek, thinly sliced
85 g (3 oz/⅔ cup) plain (all-purpose) flour
500 ml (17 fl oz/2 cups) milk
500 ml (17 fl oz/2 cups) dry white wine
125 g (4½ oz) cheddar cheese, grated
125 ml (4 fl oz/½ cup) cream
60 g (2¼ oz) parmesan cheese, grated
2 tablespoons chopped flat-leaf (Italian) parsley

Preheat the oven to 180°C (350°F/Gas 4). Line a greased shallow ovenproof dish (about 30 cm/ 12 inches square) with the lasagne sheets, gently breaking them to fill any gaps. Set aside.

Slice or pull off any vein, membrane or hard white muscle from the scallops, leaving any roe attached.

Peel the prawns and gently pull out the dark vein from each prawn back, starting from the head end. Chop the seafood and fish into even-sized pieces.

Melt the butter in a large saucepan over low heat, add the leek and cook, stirring, over medium heat for 1 minute, or until starting to soften. Stir in the flour and cook for 1 minute, or until pale and foaming. Remove from the heat and gradually stir in the combined milk and wine. Return to the heat and stir constantly over medium heat until the sauce boils and thickens. Reduce the heat and simmer for 2 minutes. Add the seafood and simmer for 1 minute. Remove from the heat, stir in the cheese, then season.

Spoon half the seafood mixture over the lasagne sheets in the dish, then top with another layer of lasagne sheets. Spoon the remaining seafood mixture over the lasagne sheets, then cover with another layer of lasagne sheets.

Pour the cream over the top, then sprinkle with the combined parmesan and parsley. Bake, uncovered, for 30 minutes, or until bubbling and golden brown.

Prawn Laksa

❀ SERVES 4–6

❀ PREPARATION TIME: 30 MINUTES

❀ COOKING TIME: 35 MINUTES

750 g (1 lb 10 oz) raw prawns (shrimp)

1½ tablespoons coriander seeds

1 tablespoon cumin seeds

1 teaspoon ground turmeric

1 onion, roughly chopped

2 teaspoons roughly chopped fresh ginger

3 garlic cloves

3 lemongrass stems, white part only, sliced

6 candlenuts or macadamia nuts, roughly
   chopped

4–6 small red chillies, roughly chopped

2–3 teaspoons shrimp paste

1 litre (35 fl oz/4 cups) chicken stock

60 ml (2 fl oz/¼ cup) vegetable oil

750 ml (26 fl oz/3 cups) coconut milk

4 fresh kaffir lime leaves

2½ tablespoons lime juice

2 tablespoons fish sauce

2 tablespoons grated palm sugar (jaggery)
   or soft brown sugar

250 g (8 oz) dried rice vermicelli

90 g (3¼ oz/1 cup) bean sprouts,
   trimmed

4 fried tofu puffs, cut into thin strips

3 tablespoons chopped Vietnamese mint

1 small handful coriander (cilantro) leaves

lime wedges, to serve

Peel the prawns, leaving the tails intact. Gently pull out the dark vein from each prawn back, starting from the head end.

Dry-fry the coriander seeds in a small frying pan over medium heat for 1–2 minutes, or until fragrant, tossing constantly. Grind finely using a mortar and pestle or spice grinder. Repeat the process with the cumin seeds.

Put the ground coriander and cumin, turmeric, onion, ginger, garlic, lemongrass, candlenuts or macadamias, chilli and shrimp paste in a food processor or blender. Add about 125 ml (4 fl oz/½ cup) of the stock and blend to a fine paste.

Heat a wok over low heat, add the oil and swirl to coat the base and side. Cook the paste for 3–5 minutes, stirring constantly. Pour in the remaining stock and bring to the boil, then reduce the heat and simmer for 15 minutes, or until reduced slightly. Add the coconut milk, kaffir lime leaves, lime juice, fish sauce and palm sugar and simmer for 5 minutes. Add the prawns and simmer for 2 minutes, or until pink and cooked. Do not boil or cover.

Meanwhile, soak the vermicelli in boiling water for 6–7 minutes, or until soft. Drain and divide among serving bowls along with most of the sprouts. Ladle on the hot soup then top with the tofu, mint, coriander and the remaining sprouts. Serve with lime wedges.

Bream with Tomato Cheese Crust

☙ SERVES 4
☙ PREPARATION TIME: 40 MINUTES
☙ COOKING TIME: 15 MINUTES

2 ripe tomatoes, peeled, seeded and finely
  chopped
1 small onion, finely chopped
1 tablespoon tomato paste (concentrated
  purée)
1/2 teaspoon ground cumin
1/2 teaspoon ground coriander
Tabasco sauce, to taste
1/4 teaspoon ground black pepper
1 tablespoon lemon juice
20 g (3/4 oz) butter, melted
4 skinless bream or red emperor fillets
90 g (31/4 oz/3/4 cup) grated cheddar cheese
40 g (11/2 oz/1/2 cup) fresh breadcrumbs
lemon wedges, to serve

Preheat the oven to 180°C (350°F/Gas 4). Lightly grease a baking tray. Put the tomato in a small bowl and mix with the onion, tomato paste, cumin, coriander and Tabasco.

Combine the pepper, lemon juice and butter in a small bowl.

Put the bream fillets on the prepared tray. Brush each fillet with the pepper mixture and top with the tomato mixture. Sprinkle with the combined cheddar and breadcrumbs and bake for 15 minutes, or until the fish is tender and flakes easily when tested with a fork. Serve with the lemon wedges.

Snapper Pies

☙ SERVES 4
☙ PREPARATION TIME: 25 MINUTES
☙ COOKING TIME: 1 HOUR 20 MINUTES

2 tablespoons olive oil
4 onions, thinly sliced
375 ml (13 fl oz/11/2 cups) fish stock
875 ml (30 fl oz/31/2 cups) cream
1 kg (2 lb 4 oz) skinless snapper fillets, cut
  into large pieces
2 sheets frozen puff pastry, thawed
1 egg, lightly beaten

Preheat the oven to 220°C (425°F/Gas 7). Heat the oil in a large frying pan, add the onion and stir over medium heat for 20 minutes, or until the onion is caramelised.

Add the fish stock, bring to the boil and cook for 10 minutes, or until the liquid is nearly evaporated. Stir in the cream and bring to the boil. Reduce the heat and simmer for 20 minutes.

Divide half the sauce among four 500 ml (17 fl oz/ 2-cup) deep ramekins or dariole moulds. Put one-quarter of the fish in each ramekin, then top with some of the remaining sauce.

Cut the pastry sheets into rounds slightly larger than the tops of the ramekins. Brush the edges of the pastry with a little of the egg. Press onto the ramekins. Brush lightly with the remaining beaten egg. Bake for 30 minutes, or until crisp, golden and puffed.

Bream with Tomato Cheese Crust

Prawn and Okra Gumbo

❧ SERVES 8

❧ PREPARATION TIME: 35 MINUTES

❧ COOKING TIME: 3 HOURS

PRAWN STOCK

1 kg (2 lb 4 oz) raw prawns (shrimp)
1 tablespoon olive oil
1 onion, chopped
1 carrot, chopped
1 celery stalk, chopped
1 bay leaf
2 whole cloves
3 garlic cloves, bruised
3 parsley stalks
1 thyme sprig
½ teaspoon black peppercorns

2 tablespoons olive oil
500 g (1 lb 2 oz) okra, thickly sliced
200 g (7 oz) chorizo, sliced
250 g (9 oz) smoked ham, diced
60 ml (2 fl oz/¼ cup) olive oil, extra
30 g (1 oz/¼ cup) plain (all-purpose) flour
2 onions, chopped
2 celery stalks, diced
1 red capsicum (pepper), diced
6 garlic cloves, finely chopped
½ teaspoon cayenne pepper
2 teaspoons sweet paprika
2 teaspoons mustard powder
large pinch ground allspice
400 g (14 oz) tomato passata (puréed
    tomatoes)
1 tablespoon tomato paste (concentrated
    purée)
2 teaspoons finely chopped thyme
2 teaspoons finely chopped oregano
2 bay leaves
2½ tablespoons worcestershire sauce
500 g (1 lb 2 oz) scallops without roe
12 oysters
chopped flat-leaf (Italian) parsley, to serve
cooked long-grain rice, to serve

To make the stock, peel the prawns, reserving the shells. Gently pull out the dark vein from each prawn back, starting at the head end. Cover the prawn meat and refrigerate until ready to use. Heat the oil in a large saucepan, add the prawn shells and cook over high heat for 8 minutes, or until bright orange. Add 2.5 litres (88 fl oz/10 cups) cold water and the remaining stock ingredients and bring to the boil. Reduce the heat to low and simmer for 30 minutes, skimming occasionally, then strain well and set aside – you should have about 2 litres (70 fl oz/8 cups) stock.

Meanwhile, heat the olive oil in a frying pan and sauté the okra over medium heat for 10 minutes, or until slightly softened. Remove from the pan and set aside. Add the chorizo to the pan and cook for 5 minutes, or until well browned, then set aside. Add the ham and cook for a few minutes, or until lightly browned.

Heat the extra olive oil in a large saucepan, add the flour and stir to combine. Cook, stirring regularly over medium heat for 30 seconds, or until the roux turns a colour somewhere between milk and dark chocolate, but do not allow to burn. Add the onion, celery, capsicum and garlic to the roux and cook for about 10 minutes, or until softened. Add the cayenne pepper, paprika, mustard and allspice and stir for 1 minute. Add the tomato passata, tomato paste, prawn stock, thyme, oregano, bay leaves, worcestershire sauce, chorizo and ham and bring to the boil. Reduce the heat to low and simmer for 1 hour, then add the okra and continue cooking for a further 1 hour or until the gumbo is thick and glossy.

Add the prawns, scallops and oysters and cook for about 5–8 minutes, or until all the seafood is cooked through. Stir in the parsley and season to taste. Ladle the soup over the hot rice in individual bowls and serve with lemon wedges, if liked.

Bouillabaisse with Rouille

❈ SERVES 6
❈ PREPARATION TIME: 35 MINUTES
❈ COOKING TIME: 1 HOUR 10 MINUTES

60 ml (2 fl oz/¼ cup) olive oil
1 large onion, chopped
2 leeks, sliced
4 garlic cloves, crushed
500 g (1 lb 2 oz) ripe tomatoes, peeled,
    seeded and roughly chopped
1–2 tablespoons tomato paste
    (concentrated purée)
6 flat-leaf (Italian) parsley sprigs
2 bay leaves
2 thyme sprigs
1 fennel sprig
2 pinches saffron threads
2 kg (4 lb 8 oz) fish trimmings (such as
    heads, bones, shellfish remains)
1 tablespoon Pernod or Ricard
4 potatoes, cut into 1.5 cm (⅝ inch) slices
1.5 kg (3 lb 5 oz) mixed fish fillets
    (such as snapper, blue eye and bream),
    cut into large chunks (see Note)
2 tablespoons chopped flat-leaf (Italian)
    parsley

TOAST
12 slices of baguette
2 large garlic cloves, sliced in half

ROUILLE
3 slices white bread, crusts removed
1 red capsicum (pepper), seeded,
    membrane removed and quartered
1 small red chilli, seeded and chopped
3 garlic cloves, crushed
1 tablespoon shredded basil
80 ml (2½ fl oz/⅓ cup) olive oil

Heat the oil in a large saucepan over medium heat, add the onion and leek and cook for 5 minutes without browning. Add the garlic, tomato and 1 tablespoon tomato paste, reduce the heat and simmer for 5 minutes. Stir in 2 litres (70 fl oz/8 cups) cold water then add the parsley, bay leaves, thyme, fennel, saffron and fish trimmings. Bring to the boil, then reduce the heat and simmer for 30 minutes. Strain the stock into a large saucepan, pressing the juices out of the ingredients and reserving 2 tablespoons of stock for the rouille.

Add the Pernod or Ricard to the saucepan and stir in the remaining tomato paste. Season, then bring to the boil and add the potato. Reduce the heat and simmer for 5 minutes. Add the firmer-fleshed fish to the saucepan and cook for 2–3 minutes, then add the more delicate pieces of fish and cook for a further 5 minutes.

Meanwhile, toast the bread until golden on both sides. While warm, rub the surfaces with the garlic.

To make the rouille, soak the bread in cold water for 5 minutes. Cook the capsicum pieces, skin side up, under a hot grill (broiler) until the skin blackens and blisters. Cool in a plastic bag, then peel. Roughly chop the flesh. Squeeze the bread dry and place in a food processor with the capsicum, chilli, garlic and basil. Process to a smooth paste. With the motor running, gradually add the oil until the consistency resembles mayonnaise. Thin with 1–2 tablespoons of the reserved stock. Season to taste.

To serve, place two pieces of toast in each soup bowl. Spoon in the soup and fish. Sprinkle with the parsley. Serve the rouille on the side.

NOTE: Use at least four different fish with a range of textures and flavours. Also, shellfish such as lobster, crab, scallops or mussels can be included.

Seafood Pie

❀ SERVES 8
❀ PREPARATION TIME: 20 MINUTES
❀ COOKING TIME: 1 HOUR 20 MINUTES

2 tablespoons olive oil
3 large onions, thinly sliced
1 fennel bulb, thinly sliced
600 ml (21 fl oz) fish stock
750 ml (26 fl oz/3 cups) cream
1 tablespoon brandy
750 g (1 lb 10 oz) skinless snapper fillets, cut into large pieces
250 g (9 oz) scallops
500 g (1 lb 2 oz) raw prawns (shrimp), peeled and deveined
2 tablespoons chopped flat-leaf (Italian) parsley
2 sheets ready-rolled puff pastry
1 egg, lightly beaten

Preheat the oven to 220°C (425°F/Gas 7). Heat the oil in a deep frying pan, add the onion and fennel and cook over medium heat for 20 minutes or until caramelised.

Add the stock to the pan and bring to the boil. Cook until the liquid is almost evaporated. Stir in the cream and brandy, bring to the boil, then reduce the heat and simmer for 10 minutes, or until reduced by half. Add the seafood and parsley and toss for 3 minutes.

Lightly grease a 2.5 litre (88 fl oz/10-cup) pie dish and add the seafood mixture. Arrange the pastry over the top to cover, trim the excess and press down around the edges. Decorate with any trimmings. Make a steam hole in the top and brush the pastry with the egg. Bake for 30 minutes, or until cooked through and the pastry is crisp and golden.

Sri Lankan Fish Fillets in Tomato Curry

❋ SERVES 6

❋ PREPARATION TIME: 20 MINUTES

❋ COOKING TIME: 20 MINUTES

60 ml (2 fl oz/¼ cup) lemon juice

60 ml (2 fl oz/¼ cup) coconut vinegar
   (see Note)

2 teaspoons cumin seeds

1 teaspoon ground turmeric

1 teaspoon cayenne pepper

1 kg (2 lb 4 oz) skinless, boneless firm
   white fish fillets

60 ml (2 fl oz/¼ cup) vegetable oil

1 large onion, finely chopped

3 large garlic cloves, crushed

2 tablespoons grated fresh ginger

1 teaspoon black mustard seeds

1.25 kg (2 lb 12 oz) tinned diced tomatoes

3 tablespoons finely chopped coriander
   (cilantro)

2 small green chillies, seeded and finely
   chopped

2 tablespoons grated palm sugar (jaggery)

steamed rice, to serve

To make the marinade, put the lemon juice, coconut vinegar, cumin seeds, turmeric, cayenne pepper and 1 teaspoon salt in a shallow, non-metallic container and mix together thoroughly.

Carefully remove any remaining bones from the fish with tweezers and cut the flesh into 2.5 x 10 cm (1 x 4 inch) pieces. Add the fish pieces to the marinade and gently toss until they are well coated. Cover with plastic wrap and refrigerate for 30 minutes.

Heat a non-stick wok over high heat, add the oil and swirl to coat the base and side. Reduce the heat to low, add the onion, garlic, ginger and mustard seeds, and cook, stirring frequently, for 5 minutes. Add the fish and marinade, the diced tomatoes, coriander, chilli and palm sugar to the wok and cover. Simmer gently, stirring occasionally, for 10–15 minutes, or until the fish is cooked and just flakes when tested with the tines of a fork. Serve with steamed rice.

NOTE: Coconut vinegar is made from the sap of various palm trees.

Poached Ocean Trout

❀ SERVES 8–10
❀ PREPARATION TIME: 50 MINUTES
❀ COOKING TIME: 50 MINUTES

2 litres (70 fl oz/8 cups) white wine
60 ml (2 fl oz/¼ cup) white wine vinegar
2 onions
10 whole cloves
4 carrots, chopped
1 lemon, cut in quarters
2 bay leaves
4 flat-leaf (Italian) parsley stalks
1 teaspoon whole black peppercorns
2.5 kg (5 lb 8 oz) ocean trout, cleaned,
    gutted and scaled
fresh chives, to garnish
1 lemon, thinly sliced, to garnish

DILL MAYONNAISE
1 egg, at room temperature
1 egg yolk, at room temperature
1 tablespoon lemon juice
1 teaspoon white wine vinegar
375 ml (13 fl oz/1½ cups) light olive oil
1–2 tablespoons chopped dill

Combine the wine and vinegar in a large heavy-based saucepan with 2.5 litres (88 fl oz/10 cups) water.

Stud the onions with the cloves. Add to the pan with the carrot, lemon, bay leaves, parsley and peppercorns. Bring to the boil, reduce the heat and simmer for 30–35 minutes. Cool. Strain into a fish kettle that will hold the trout.

Place the whole fish in the fish kettle and add water if necessary, to just cover the fish. Bring to the boil, then reduce the heat to a low simmer, cover and poach gently for 10–15 minutes, until the fish flakes when tested in the thickest part. Remove the kettle from the heat and leave the fish to cool in the liquid.

For the dill mayonnaise, process the egg, yolk, lemon juice and wine vinegar in a food processor for 10 seconds, or until blended. With the motor running, add the oil in a thin, steady stream, blending until all the oil is added and the mayonnaise is thick and creamy – it should be thick enough to form peaks. Transfer to a bowl and stir in the dill and salt and pepper, to taste.

Remove the cold fish from the liquid, place on a serving platter and peel back the skin. Garnish with chives and lemon slices. Serve with the dill mayonnaise.

NOTE: Atlantic salmon, snapper, sea bass or red emperor can also be used. If you don't have a fish kettle, use a baking dish big enough to hold the fish, cover with foil and bake in a 180°C (350°F/Gas 4) oven for 20–30 minutes.

Seafood Risotto

❀ SERVES 4–6
❀ PREPARATION TIME: 25 MINUTES
❀ COOKING TIME: 45 MINUTES

500 g (1 lb 2 oz) black mussels
310 ml (10¾ fl oz/1¼ cups) dry white
  wine
1.25 litres (44 fl oz/5 cups) fish stock
pinch saffron threads
2 tablespoons olive oil
30 g (1 oz) butter
500 g (1 lb 2 oz) raw prawns (shrimp),
  peeled and deveined
225 g (8 oz) squid tubes, sliced into
  thin rings
200 g (7 oz) scallops
3 garlic cloves, crushed
1 onion, finely chopped
440 g (15½ oz/2 cups) risotto rice
2 ripe tomatoes, peeled and roughly
  chopped
2 tablespoons chopped flat-leaf (Italian)
  parsley

Scrub the mussels with a stiff brush and pull out the hairy beards. Discard any broken mussels, or open ones that don't close when tapped. Rinse well. Pour the wine into a large saucepan and bring to the boil. Add the mussels and cook, covered, over medium heat for 3–5 minutes, or until the mussels open. Discard any unopened mussels. Strain, reserving the liquid. Remove the mussels from their shells. Combine the mussel liquid, stock and saffron in a saucepan, cover and keep at a low simmer.

Heat the oil and butter in a saucepan over medium heat. Add the prawns and cook until pink. Remove. Add the squid and scallops and cook about 1–2 minutes, or until white. Remove. Add the garlic and onion and cook for 3 minutes, or until golden. Add the rice and stir. Add 125 ml (4 fl oz/½ cup) of the hot liquid, stirring until it is all absorbed. Continue adding liquid, 125 ml (4 fl oz/½ cup) at a time, stirring, for 25 minutes, or until the liquid is absorbed. Stir in the tomato, seafood and parsley and heat through. Season to taste.

Balinese Seafood Curry

⚜ PREPARATION TIME: 20 MINUTES

⚜ COOKING TIME: 20 MINUTES

CURRY PASTE

2 tomatoes, peeled, seeded and roughly
    chopped
5 small red chillies, seeded and chopped
5 garlic cloves, chopped
2 lemongrass stems, white part only, sliced
1 tablespoon coriander seeds, dry-roasted
    and ground
1 teaspoon shrimp powder, dry-roasted
    (see Notes)
1 tablespoon ground almonds
1/4 teaspoon ground nutmeg
1 teaspoon ground turmeric
3 tablespoons tamarind purée

400 g (14 oz) raw prawns (shrimp)
1 tablespoon lime juice
250 g (9 oz) swordfish, cut into 3 cm
    (1 1/4 inch) cubes
250 g (9 oz) calamari tubes, cut into
    1 cm (1/2 inch) rings
60 ml (2 fl oz/1/4 cup) vegetable oil
2 red onions, chopped
2 small red chillies, seeded and sliced
125 ml (4 fl oz/1/2 cup) fish stock
shredded Thai basil, to garnish

To make the curry paste, put the ingredients in a food processor and blend until a thick paste forms.

Peel the prawns and gently pull out the dark vein from each prawn back, starting at the head end.

Pour the lime juice into a bowl and season. Add the fish, prawns and calamari, coat well and allow to marinate for 20 minutes.

Heat a non-stick wok over high heat, add the oil and swirl to coat the base and side. Add the onion, chilli and curry paste, and cook, stirring occasionally, over low heat for 10 minutes, or until fragrant. Add the swordfish and prawns, and stir to coat in the curry paste mixture. Cook for 3 minutes, or until the prawns just turn pink, then add the calamari and cook for a further 1 minute. Add the stock and bring to the boil, then reduce the heat and simmer for 2 minutes, or until the seafood is cooked and tender. Season to taste and garnish with the basil.

NOTES: If you can't find shrimp powder, put some dried shrimp in a mortar and pestle or small food processor and grind or process into a fine powder.
   Use a non-stick or stainless steel wok to cook this recipe as the tamarind will react with the metal in a regular wok and badly taint the flavour of the dish.

Seared Scallops with Chilli Bean Paste

❀ SERVES 4
❀ PREPARATION TIME: 20 MINUTES
❀ COOKING TIME: 15 MINUTES

500 g (1 lb 2 oz) hokkien (egg) noodles
60 ml (2 fl oz/¼ cup) peanut oil
20 scallops, roe removed
1 large onion, cut into thin wedges
3 garlic cloves, crushed
1 tablespoon grated fresh ginger
1 tablespoon chilli bean paste
150 g (5½ oz) choy sum, cut into 5 cm
   (2 inch) lengths
60 ml (2 fl oz/¼ cup) chicken stock
2 tablespoons light soy sauce
2 tablespoons kecap manis
1 handful coriander (cilantro) leaves
90 g (3¼ oz/1 cup) bean sprouts, washed
1 large red chilli, seeded and thinly sliced
1 teaspoon sesame oil
1 tablespoon Chinese rice wine

Put the noodles in a heatproof bowl, cover with boiling water and soak for 1 minute to separate. Drain, rinse, then drain again. Set aside.

Heat a wok over high heat, add 2 tablespoons peanut oil and swirl to coat the base and side. Add the scallops in batches and sear for 20 seconds on each side, or until sealed. Remove from the wok and set aside.

Add the remaining peanut oil to the wok and swirl to coat. Stir-fry the onion for 1–2 minutes, or until softened. Add the garlic and ginger and cook for 30 seconds. Stir in the chilli bean paste and cook for 1 minute, or until fragrant. Add the choy sum, noodles, stock, soy sauce and kecap manis. Stir-fry for 4 minutes, or until the choy sum has wilted and the noodles have absorbed most of the liquid. Return the scallops to the wok, add the coriander, bean sprouts, chilli, sesame oil and rice wine, tossing gently until combined. Serve immediately.

Indonesian Sambal Squid

❊ SERVES 6

❊ PREPARATION TIME: 20 MINUTES

❊ COOKING TIME: 15 MINUTES

1 kg (2 lb 4 oz) cleaned squid hoods
1 tablespoon white vinegar
1 tablespoon tamarind pulp
80 ml (2½ fl oz/⅓ cup) boiling water
4 red Asian shallots or French shallots,
    finely chopped
8 small red chillies, half of them seeded,
    chopped
6 garlic cloves
1 lemongrass stem, white part only,
    chopped
2 teaspoons grated fresh ginger
½ teaspoon shrimp paste
2½ tablespoons peanut oil
½ teaspoon ground cumin
1½ tablespoons grated palm sugar
    (jaggery) or soft brown sugar
steamed rice, to serve

Cut each squid hood in half lengthways and open out flat, with the inside uppermost. Score a shallow diamond pattern all over the squid hoods, taking care not to cut all the way through. Cut the hoods into 5 cm (2 inch) squares. Put the pieces in a bowl with the vinegar and 1 litre (35 fl oz/4 cups) water and soak for 10 minutes, then rinse and drain the squid and set aside.

Put the tamarind in a bowl and pour in the boiling water. Allow to steep for 5 minutes, breaking up the pulp as it softens. Strain into a bowl and discard the solids.

Put the shallots, chilli, garlic, lemongrass, ginger, shrimp paste and 1 teaspoon of the oil in a small food processor or mortar and pestle and blend or pound until a smooth paste is formed. Stir in the cumin.

Heat a non-stick wok over high heat, add 1 tablespoon of the oil and swirl to coat the base and side. Add the paste and cook for 5 minutes, or until it is fragrant, glossy and the liquid has evaporated. Remove from the wok.

Reheat the wok to very hot, add the remaining oil and swirl to coat. Add the squid pieces in small batches and stir-fry for 1–2 minutes, or until cooked through. Remove from the wok.

Reduce the heat to medium, then add the paste, strained tamarind water and palm sugar. Stir-fry for 2 minutes, or until the sauce ingredients are well combined. Return the squid to the wok and stir-fry for 1 minute, or until the squid is well coated with the sauce and heated through. Serve with steamed rice.

NOTE: Use a non-stick or stainless steel wok to cook this recipe because the tamarind will react with the metal in a regular wok and taint the flavour of the dish.

Cioppino

❊ SERVES 4
❊ PREPARATION TIME: 30 MINUTES
❊ COOKING TIME: 50 MINUTES

2 dried Chinese mushrooms
1 kg (2 lb 4 oz) skinless firm white fish
    fillets (such as hake, snapper, ocean
    perch or red mullet)
375 g (13 oz) raw large prawns (shrimp)
1 raw lobster tail (about 400 g/14 oz)
12–15 black mussels
60 ml (2 fl oz/¼ cup) olive oil
1 large onion, finely chopped
1 green capsicum (pepper), seeded and
    membrane removed, finely chopped
2–3 garlic cloves, crushed
425 g (15 oz) tinned crushed tomatoes
250 ml (9 fl oz/1 cup) dry white wine
250 ml (9 fl oz/1 cup) tomato juice
250 ml (9 fl oz/1 cup) fish stock
1 bay leaf
2 flat-leaf (Italian) parsley sprigs
2 teaspoons shredded basil
1 tablespoon chopped flat-leaf (Italian)
    parsley, to garnish

Place the mushrooms in a small bowl, cover with boiling water and soak for 20 minutes. Cut the fish into bite-sized pieces, removing any bones.

Peel the prawns, leaving the tails intact. Gently pull out the dark vein from each prawn back, starting at the head end.

Starting at the end where the head was, cut down the sides of the lobster shell on the underside of the lobster with kitchen scissors. Pull back the flap, remove the meat from the shell and cut into small pieces.

Scrub the mussels with a stiff brush and pull out the hairy beards. Discard any broken mussels, or open ones that don't close when tapped on the bench. Rinse well.

Drain the mushrooms, squeeze dry and chop finely. Heat the oil in a heavy-based saucepan, add the onion, capsicum and garlic and stir over medium heat for about 5 minutes, or until the onion is soft. Add the mushrooms, tomato, wine, tomato juice, stock, bay leaf, parsley sprigs and basil. Bring to the boil, reduce the heat, then cover and simmer for 30 minutes.

Layer the fish and prawns in a large frying pan. Add the sauce, then cover and leave on low heat for 10 minutes, or until the prawns are pink and the fish is cooked. Add the lobster and mussels and simmer for a further 4–5 minutes. Season. Discard any unopened mussels. Sprinkle with the chopped parsley.

Fish Baked in Salt

❀ SERVES 6
❀ PREPARATION TIME: 20 MINUTES
❀ COOKING TIME: 40 MINUTES

1.8 kg (4 lb) whole fish (such as blue-eye,
    jewfish, sea bass, or groper), scaled
    and cleaned
2 lemons, sliced
4 thyme sprigs, plus extra, to garnish
1 fennel bulb, thinly sliced
3 kg (6 lb 12 oz) rock salt
100 g (3½ oz) plain (all-purpose) flour

Preheat the oven to 200°C (400°F/Gas 6). Rinse the fish and pat dry inside and out with paper towel. Place the lemon, thyme and fennel inside the cavity.

Pack half the salt into a large baking dish and place the fish on top. Cover with the remaining salt, pressing down until the salt is packed firmly around the fish.

Combine the flour with enough water to form a smooth paste, then brush, spreading carefully and evenly, over the surface of the salt. Be careful not to disturb the salt.

Bake the fish for 30–40 minutes, or until a skewer inserted into the centre of the fish comes out hot. Carefully crack open the salt crust with the back of a spoon and gently remove the skin from the fish, ensuring that no salt remains on the flesh. Garnish with thyme.

Stuffed Fish

❀ SERVES 4
❀ PREPARATION TIME: 40 MINUTES
❀ COOKING TIME: 45 MINUTES

1 kg (2 lb 4 oz) whole fish (such as
    snapper, murray cod, or sea bass),
    scaled and cleaned
60 ml (2 fl oz/¼ cup) lemon juice
30 g (1 oz) butter, chopped

STUFFING
2 tablespoons olive oil
1 small onion, finely chopped
3 tablespoons chopped celery leaves
2 tablespoons chopped flat-leaf (Italian)
    parsley
80 g (2¾ oz/1 cup) fresh breadcrumbs
1½ tablespoons lemon juice
1 egg, lightly beaten

Preheat the oven to 180°C (350°F/Gas 4). Pat the fish dry and sprinkle with salt and the lemon juice. Set aside.

To make the stuffing, heat the oil in a saucepan, add the onion and cook over medium heat for 2 minutes, or until softened. Add the celery leaves and parsley and cook, stirring, for a further 2 minutes. Spoon into a bowl, add the breadcrumbs, lemon juice and salt, to taste, then mix well. Cool slightly, then stir in the egg.

Place the stuffing in the fish cavity and secure the opening with skewers. Place the fish in a large greased baking dish and dot with butter. Bake for 30–35 minutes, or until the fish is cooked and flakes easily when tested with a fork. The thickness of the fish will determine the cooking time. Transfer to a serving dish.

Fish Baked in Salt

Salmon Nabe

❀ SERVES 2–4

❀ PREPARATION TIME: 20 MINUTES

❀ COOKING TIME: 40 MINUTES

12 dried shiitake mushrooms

250 g (9 oz) firm tofu

1/2 Chinese cabbage (wong bok)

4 salmon cutlets

2 x 5 cm (2 inch) pieces tinned bamboo
    shoots

2 litres (70 fl oz/8 cups) dashi

80 ml (2 1/2 fl oz/1/3 cup) shoyu (Japanese
    soy sauce)

60 ml (2 fl oz/1/4 cup) mirin or sake

SESAME SEED SAUCE

100 g (3 1/2 oz) white sesame seeds

2 teaspoons oil

125 ml (4 fl oz/1/2 cup) shoyu
    (Japanese soy sauce)

2 tablespoons mirin

3 teaspoons caster (superfine) sugar

1/2 teaspoon instant dashi granules

Soak the mushrooms in warm water for 15 minutes, then drain. Cut the tofu into 12 squares. Coarsely shred the cabbage into 5 cm (2 inch) wide pieces.

Place the mushrooms, tofu, cabbage, salmon, bamboo shoots, dashi, shoyu, mirin or sake and a pinch of salt in a large saucepan and bring to the boil. Reduce the heat, cover and simmer over medium heat for 15 minutes. Turn the salmon cutlets over and simmer for a further 15 minutes, or until tender.

To make the sesame seed sauce, toast the sesame seeds in a frying pan over medium heat for 3–4 minutes, shaking the pan gently, until the seeds are golden brown. Remove from the pan at once to prevent burning. Grind the seeds using a mortar and pestle until a paste is formed. Add the oil, if necessary, to assist in forming a paste. Mix the paste with the shoyu, mirin, sugar, dashi granules and 125 ml (4 fl oz/ 1/2 cup) warm water.

Pour the salmon nabe into warmed serving bowls and serve with the sesame seed sauce.

NOTE: This dish is traditionally cooked in a clay pot over a burner and served in the same pot. Diners dip the fish and vegetable pieces into the accompanying sauce and the broth is served in small bowls at the end of the meal.

Salmon Steaks with Herb Sauce

❀ SERVES 4

❀ PREPARATION TIME: 25 MINUTES

❀ COOKING TIME: 20 MINUTES

2 tablespoons olive oil
4 salmon steaks (250 g/9 oz each)

HERB SAUCE
375 ml (13 fl oz/1 ½ cups) fish stock
125 ml (4 fl oz/½ cup) white wine
3 tablespoons snipped chives
3 tablespoons chopped flat-leaf (Italian)
    parsley
2 tablespoons shredded basil
2 tablespoons chopped tarragon
250 ml (9 fl oz/1 cup) cream
2 egg yolks

To make the herb sauce, combine the stock and wine in a saucepan and bring to the boil. Boil for 5 minutes or until the liquid has reduced by half. Transfer to a food processor, add the chives, parsley, basil and tarragon and process for 30 seconds. Return to the pan, then stir in the cream and bring to the boil. Reduce the heat to low and simmer for 5 minutes, or until reduced by half. Place the egg yolks in a food processor and process until smooth. Drizzle in the herb mixture. Process until smooth. Season.

Heat the oil in a frying pan, add the salmon steaks and cook over medium heat for 3 minutes each side, or until just cooked through. Serve hot with herb sauce.

Tandoori Fish Cutlets

※ SERVES 4

※ PREPARATION TIME: 15 MINUTES

※ COOKING TIME: 10 MINUTES

4 firm white fish cutlets (such as blue-eye,
    snapper or perch)
60 ml (2 fl oz/¼ cup) lemon juice
1 onion, finely chopped
2 garlic cloves, crushed
1 tablespoon grated fresh ginger
1 red chilli
1 tablespoon garam masala
1 teaspoon paprika
500 g (1 lb 2 oz/2 cups) Greek-style
    yoghurt, plus extra to serve
few drops red food colouring (optional)
baby English spinach leaves, to serve
lime wedges, to serve

Pat the fish cutlets dry with paper towels and arrange in a shallow non-metallic dish. Drizzle the lemon juice over the fish and turn to coat the cutlets with the juice.

Blend the onion, garlic, ginger, chilli, garam masala, paprika and a pinch of salt in a blender until smooth. Transfer to a bowl and stir in the yoghurt and the food colouring, if using. Spoon the marinade over the fish and turn the fish to coat thoroughly. Cover and refrigerate overnight.

Heat a barbecue hotplate. Remove the cutlets from the marinade and allow any excess to drip off. Cook the cutlets on the barbecue, or under a grill (broiler), for 3–4 minutes each side, or until the fish flakes easily when tested with a fork. Serve with extra yoghurt, English spinach leaves and lime wedges.

Skewered Swordfish with Lemon Sauce

※ SERVES 6

※ PREPARATION TIME: 15 MINUTES

※ COOKING TIME: 5 MINUTES

MARINADE
80 ml (2½ fl oz/⅓ cup) lemon juice
2 tablespoons olive oil
1 small red onion, thinly sliced
1 teaspoon paprika
2 bay leaves, crushed
10 sage leaves, torn

1.5 kg (3 lb 5 oz) swordfish
3 tablespoons chopped flat-leaf (Italian)
    parsley
60 ml (2 fl oz/¼ cup) olive oil
60 ml (2 fl oz/¼ cup) lemon juice

Combine the marinade ingredients with 1 teaspoon salt and some ground black pepper in a bowl. Add the fish, toss to coat with the marinade, then cover and refrigerate for 3 hours, turning the fish occasionally.

Cut the fish into 3 cm (1¼ inch) cubes. Thread onto six metal skewers and cook on a chargrill pan or barbecue hotplate for 5 minutes, turning and brushing with marinade several times.

To make the lemon sauce, combine the parsley, oil and lemon juice. Serve over the fish.

Tandoori Fish Cutlets

Salmon Pie

✾ SERVES 4–6

✾ PREPARATION TIME: 25 MINUTES

✾ COOKING TIME: 1 HOUR

60 g (2¼ oz) butter

1 onion, finely chopped

200 g (7 oz) button mushrooms, sliced

2 tablespoons lemon juice

200 g (7 oz) cooked poached salmon fillet,
  broken into small pieces, or
  220 g (7¾ oz) tinned red salmon

2 hard-boiled eggs, chopped

2 tablespoons chopped dill

3 tablespoons chopped flat-leaf (Italian)
  parsley

185 g (6½ oz/1 cup) cooked long-grain
  brown rice

60 ml (2 fl oz/¼ cup) cream

375 g (13 oz) ready-made frozen puff
  pastry, thawed

1 egg, lightly beaten

sour cream, to serve (optional)

Melt half the butter in a frying pan and cook the onion for 5 minutes until soft but not brown. Add the mushroom and cook for 5 minutes. Stir in the lemon juice, then remove from the pan.

Melt the remaining butter in the pan, add the salmon and stir for 2 minutes. Remove from the heat, cool slightly and add the egg, dill, parsley, and salt and pepper, to taste. Mix gently and set aside.

Mix the rice and cream in a small bowl.

Roll out half the pastry to 15 x 25 cm (6 x 10 inches). Trim the pastry neatly, saving the trimmings, and put on a greased baking tray.

Layer the filling onto the pastry, leaving a 3 cm (1¼ inch) border. Put half the rice into the centre of the pastry, then the salmon and egg mixture, followed by the mushroom, then the remaining rice. Brush the pastry border with the egg.

Roll out the other pastry half to 20 x 30 cm (8 x 12 inches) and place over the filling. Seal the edges. Make two slits in the top. Decorate with the trimmings and chill for 30 minutes.

Preheat the oven to 200°C (400°F/Gas 6). Brush the pie with the egg and bake for 15 minutes. Reduce the oven to 180°C (350°F/Gas 4) and bake the pie for 25–30 minutes, or until crisp and golden. Serve with sour cream.

NOTE: You will need to cook about 100 g (3½ oz/½ cup) brown rice for this recipe.

Barbecued Fish with Onions and Ginger

* SERVES 4–6
* PREPARATION TIME: 25 MINUTES
* COOKING TIME: 25 MINUTES

1 kg (2 lb 4 oz) small whole firm white
    fish, cleaned, gutted and scaled
2 teaspoons bottled green peppercorns,
    drained and finely crushed
2 teaspoons chopped red chilli
3 teaspoons fish sauce
60 ml (2 fl oz/¼ cup) vegetable oil
2 onions, thinly sliced
4 cm (1½ inch) piece fresh ginger,
    thinly sliced
3 garlic cloves, cut into very thin slivers
2 teaspoons sugar
4 spring onions (scallions), finely shredded

LEMON AND GARLIC DIPPING SAUCE
60 ml (2 fl oz/¼ cup) lemon juice
2 tablespoons fish sauce
1 tablespoon caster (superfine) sugar
2 small red chillies, finely chopped
3 garlic cloves, chopped

Wash the fish and pat dry inside and out with paper towels. Cut two or three diagonal slashes into the thickest part on both sides. In a food processor, process the peppercorns, chilli and fish sauce to a paste and brush over the fish. Refrigerate for 20 minutes.

Heat a barbecue hotplate or grill (broiler) until very hot and then brush with 1 tablespoon of the oil. Cook the fish for 8 minutes each side, or until the flesh flakes easily. If grilling (broiling), don't cook too close to the heat.

While the fish is cooking, heat the remaining oil in a frying pan and stir the onion over medium heat until golden. Add the ginger, garlic and sugar and cook for 3 minutes. Serve over the fish. Sprinkle with spring onion.

Stir all the dipping sauce ingredients in a bowl until the sugar has dissolved. Serve with the fish.

Fish Cooked in Paper

* SERVES 4
* PREPARATION TIME: 20 MINUTES
* COOKING TIME: 20 MINUTES

4 skinless firm white fish fillets (200 g/
    7 oz each)
1 leek, white part only, cut into thin
    batons
4 spring onions (scallions), shredded
30 g (1 oz) butter, softened
1 lemon, cut into 12 very thin slices
2–3 tablespoons lemon juice

Preheat the oven to 180°C (350°F/Gas 4). Place each fish fillet in the centre of a piece of baking paper large enough to enclose the fish. Season lightly.

Scatter the leek and spring onion over the fish. Top each with a teaspoon of butter and three slices of lemon. Sprinkle with the lemon juice. Bring the paper together and fold over several times. Fold the ends under. Bake on a baking tray for 20 minutes (the steam will make the paper puff up), or until the fish flakes easily when tested with a fork. Serve as parcels or lift the fish out and pour the juices over the top before serving.

Barbecued Fish with Onions and Ginger

Spanish-Style Rice, Mussel, Prawn and Chorizo Soup

❀ SERVES 4
❀ PREPARATION TIME: 45 MINUTES
❀ COOKING TIME: 45 MINUTES

500 g (1 lb 2 oz) raw prawns (shrimp)
1 kg (2 lb 4 oz) black mussels
250 ml (9 fl oz/1 cup) dry sherry
1 tablespoon olive oil
1 red onion, chopped
200 g (7 oz) chorizo sausage, thinly sliced
4 garlic cloves, crushed
100 g (3½ oz/½ cup) long-grain rice
400 g (14 oz) tinned chopped tomatoes
2 litres (70 fl oz/8 cups) chicken stock
½ teaspoon saffron threads
2 bay leaves
1 tablespoon chopped oregano
3 tablespoons chopped flat-leaf (Italian) parsley

Peel the prawns, leaving the tails intact. Gently pull out the dark vein from each prawn back, starting from the head end. Scrub the mussels with a stiff brush and pull out the hairy beards. Discard any broken mussels or open ones that don't close when tapped on the bench. Rinse well.

Put the mussels in a saucepan with the sherry and cook, covered, over high heat for 3 minutes, or until the mussels have opened. Strain the liquid into a bowl and reserve. Discard any unopened mussels. Remove all but eight mussels from their shells and discard the empty shells.

Heat the oil in a large saucepan over medium heat, add the onion and cook for 5 minutes, or until softened but not browned. Add the chorizo and cook for 3–5 minutes, or until browned. Add the garlic and cook for a further 1 minute. Add the rice and stir to coat with the chorizo mixture. Add the reserved cooking liquid and cook for 1 minute before adding the tomato, stock, saffron, bay leaves and oregano. Bring to the boil then reduce the heat and simmer, covered, for 25 minutes.

Add the prawns and the mussels (except the ones in their shells) to the soup, cover with a lid, and cook for 3 minutes then stir in the parsley. Ladle into four serving bowls, then top each bowl with two mussels still in their shells.

Tuna Skewers with Moroccan Spices

※ SERVES 4
※ PREPARATION TIME: 20 MINUTES
※ COOKING TIME: 5 MINUTES

800 g (1 lb 12 oz) tuna steaks
2 tablespoons olive oil
1/2 teaspoon ground cumin
2 teaspoons finely grated lemon zest

CHERMOULA
1/2 teaspoon ground coriander
3 teaspoons ground cumin
2 teaspoons paprika
pinch cayenne pepper
4 garlic cloves, crushed
15 g (1/2 oz) chopped flat-leaf (Italian) parsley
25 g (1/4 oz) chopped coriander (cilantro) leaves
80 ml (2 1/2 fl oz/1/3 cup) lemon juice
125 ml (4 fl oz/1/2 cup) olive oil
couscous, to serve

If using wooden skewers, soak for about 30 minutes to prevent them from burning during cooking.

Cut the tuna into 3 cm (1 1/4 inch) cubes and put in a shallow non-metallic dish. Combine the oil, cumin and lemon zest and pour over the tuna. Toss to coat, then cover and marinate in the refrigerator for 10 minutes.

Meanwhile, to make the chermoula, put the ground coriander, cumin, paprika and cayenne pepper in a small frying pan and cook over medium heat for 30 seconds, or until fragrant. Combine with the remaining chermoula ingredients and set aside.

Thread the tuna onto the skewers. Lightly oil a chargrill pan or barbecue hotplate and cook the skewers for 1 minute on each side for rare or 2 minutes for medium. Serve the skewers on a bed of couscous with the chermoula drizzled over the tuna.

Trout with Almonds

※ SERVES 2
※ PREPARATION TIME: 25 MINUTES
※ COOKING TIME: 10 MINUTES

2 whole rainbow trout, or baby salmon,
    clean, gutted and scaled
plain (all-purpose) flour, for coating
60 g (2 1/4 oz) butter
25 g (1 oz/1/4 cup) flaked almonds
2 tablespoons lemon juice
1 tablespoon finely chopped flat-leaf
    (Italian) parsley
lemon or lime wedges, to serve

Wash the fish and pat dry with paper towels. Open the fish out, skin side up. Run a rolling pin along the backbone, starting at the tail, pressing down gently. Turn the fish over and use scissors to cut through the backbone at each end of the fish. Lift out the backbone. Remove any remaining bones. Trim the fins with scissors. Coat the fish with flour. In a large frying pan, heat half the butter and add the fish. Cook for 4 minutes each side, or until golden brown. Remove the fish and place on heated serving plates. Cover with foil.

Heat the remaining butter, add the almonds and stir until light golden. Add the lemon juice, parsley, and salt and freshly ground pepper. Stir until the sauce is heated through. Pour over the fish and serve with lemon or lime wedges.

Tuna Skewers with Moroccan Spices

Sweet Chilli Prawns

※ SERVES 4
※ PREPARATION TIME: 20 MINUTES
※ COOKING TIME: 10 MINUTES

80 ml (2 1/2 fl oz/ 1/3 cup) chilli garlic
    sauce
2 tablespoons tomato sauce (ketchup)
2 tablespoons Chinese rice wine
1 tablespoon Chinese black vinegar
1 tablespoon soy sauce
1 tablespoon soft brown sugar
1 teaspoon cornflour (cornstarch)
1 kg (2 lb 4 oz) raw prawns (shrimp)
2 tablespoons peanut oil
3 cm (1 1/4 inch) piece fresh ginger,
    finely sliced
2 garlic cloves, finely chopped
5 spring onions (scallions), cut into 3 cm
    (1 1/4 inch) lengths
finely chopped spring onion (scallion),
    to garnish
steamed rice, to serve

To make the stir-fry sauce, combine the chilli garlic sauce, tomato sauce, rice wine, black vinegar, soy sauce and sugar in a small bowl. Dissolve the cornflour in 125 ml (4 fl oz/ 1/2 cup) water and stir into the sauce. Set aside.

Peel the prawns and gently pull out the dark vein from each prawn back, starting from the head end.

Heat a wok over high heat, add the oil and swirl to coat the base and side, then add the ginger, garlic and spring onion and stir-fry for 1 minute. Add the prawns and cook for 2 minutes, or until the prawns are pink and starting to curl. Remove from the wok.

Pour the stir-fry sauce into the wok and cook, stirring, for 1–2 minutes, or until it thickens slightly. Return the prawns to the wok for a further 2 minutes, or until heated and cooked through. Garnish with the chopped spring onion. Serve with steamed rice.

Stir~Fried Fish with Ginger

※ SERVES 4
※ PREPARATION TIME: 20 MINUTES
※ COOKING TIME: 15 MINUTES

1 tablespoon peanut oil
1 small onion, thinly sliced
3 teaspoons ground coriander
600 g (1 lb 5 oz) boneless white fish
    fillets, cut into bite-sized strips
1 tablespoon finely shredded fresh ginger
1 teaspoon finely chopped and seeded
    green chilli
2 tablespoons lime juice
2 tablespoons coriander (cilantro) leaves
steamed rice, to serve

Heat a wok over high heat, add the oil and swirl to coat the base and side. Add the onion and stir-fry for 4 minutes, or until soft and golden. Add the ground coriander and cook for 1–2 minutes, or until fragrant. Add the fish, ginger and chilli and stir-fry for 5–7 minutes, or until the fish is cooked through, taking care that the fish doesn't break up. Stir in the lime juice and season to taste. Garnish with the coriander leaves and serve with steamed rice.

Sweet Chilli Prawns

Baked Salmon

2 kg (4 lb 8 oz) Atlantic salmon, cleaned,
    gutted and scaled
2 spring onions (scallions), roughly
    chopped
3 dill sprigs
1/2 lemon, thinly sliced
6 black peppercorns
olive oil, for brushing
60 ml (2 fl oz/1/4 cup) dry white wine
3 bay leaves
lemon wedges, to serve
dill sprigs, to garnish

Preheat the oven to 180°C (350°F/Gas 4). Rinse the salmon under cold running water and pat dry inside and out with paper towels. Stuff the cavity with the spring onion, dill, lemon slices and peppercorns.

Brush a large double-layered piece of foil with oil and lay the salmon on the foil. Sprinkle the wine all over the salmon and arrange the bay leaves over the top. Fold the foil over and wrap up tightly.

Bake in a shallow baking dish for 30 minutes. Turn the oven off and leave the salmon in the oven, with the foil on, for 45 minutes with the door closed.

Undo the foil and carefully peel away the skin of the salmon on the top side. Carefully flip the salmon onto the serving plate. Remove the skin from the other side. Pull out the fins and any visible bones. Serve at room temperature with lemon wedges. Garnish with dill.

Jasmine Tea Steamed Fish

❀ SERVES 4
❀ PREPARATION TIME: 10 MINUTES
❀ COOKING TIME: 25 MINUTES

200 g (7 oz) jasmine tea leaves
100 g (3 1/2 oz) fresh ginger, thinly sliced
4 spring onions (scallions), cut into 5 cm
    (2 inch) lengths
4 x 200 g (7 oz) skinless firm white
    fish fillets

GINGER SPRING ONION SAUCE
125 ml (4 fl oz/1/2 cup) fish stock
60 ml (2 fl oz/1/4 cup) light soy sauce
3 spring onions (scallions), thinly sliced
1 tablespoon finely shredded fresh ginger
2 teaspoons caster (superfine) sugar
1 large red chilli, sliced

Line a double bamboo steamer with baking paper. Place the tea, ginger and spring onion in a layer on the bottom steamer basket. Cover and steam over a wok of simmering water for 10 minutes, or until the tea is moist and fragrant.

Lay the fish in a single layer in the top steamer basket and steam for 5–10 minutes, or until the fish flakes easily when tested with a fork.

To make the ginger spring onion sauce, combine all the ingredients in a saucepan with 125 ml (4 fl oz/1/2 cup) water. Heat over low heat for 5 minutes, or until the sugar has dissolved. Drizzle the fish with the sauce and serve with steamed rice, if desired.

Baked Salmon

Chorba Bil Hout

❀ SERVES 6
❀ PREPARATION TIME: 30 MINUTES
❀ COOKING TIME: 30 MINUTES

2 red capsicums (peppers), quartered,
    seeded and membrane removed
1 long fresh red chilli, seeded
2 tablespoons extra virgin olive oil
1 brown onion, finely chopped
1 tablespoon tomato paste (concentrated
    purée)
2–3 teaspoons harissa
4 garlic cloves, finely chopped
2 teaspoons ground cumin
750 ml (26 fl oz/3 cups) fish stock
400 g (14 oz) tinned crushed tomatoes
750 g (1 lb 10 oz) skinless firm white fish
    fillets (such as blue eye or ling),
    cut into 2 cm (³⁄₄ inch) squares
2 bay leaves
2 tablespoons chopped coriander (cilantro)
    leaves
6 thick slices of baguette
1 garlic clove, halved

Grill (broil) the capsicum and chilli until the skin is blackened and blistered. Cool in a plastic bag then peel and cut into thin strips.

Heat the oil in a large saucepan and cook the onion for 5 minutes, or until softened. Add the tomato paste, harissa, chopped garlic, cumin and 125 ml (4 fl oz/ ¹⁄₂ cup) water then stir to combine. Add the fish stock, tomatoes and 500 ml (17 fl oz/2 cups) water. Bring to the boil, then reduce the heat and add the fish and bay leaves. Simmer for 7–8 minutes, or until the fish is just cooked. Remove the fish with a slotted spoon and place on a plate. Discard the bay leaves. When the soup has cooled slightly, add half the chopped coriander and purée in batches, in a food processor, until smooth. Season to taste.

Return the soup to the pan, add the fish, capsicum and chilli and simmer gently while you prepare the toast.

Toast the bread and, while still warm, rub with the cut garlic. Place one slice of toast in each soup bowl and pile several pieces of fish on top. Ladle the soup over the top, distributing the capsicum evenly. Garnish with the remaining coriander.

poultry

Roasted Rosemary Chicken

※ SERVES 4
※ PREPARATION TIME: 15 MINUTES
※ COOKING TIME: 1 HOUR

1.5–1.8 kg (3 lb 5 oz–4 lb) chicken
6 large rosemary sprigs
4 garlic cloves
60 ml (2 fl oz/¼ cup) olive oil

Preheat the oven to 220°C (425°F/Gas 7). Wipe the chicken inside and out and pat dry with paper towels. Season the chicken cavity and place four rosemary sprigs and the garlic cloves inside.

Rub the outside of the chicken with 1 tablespoon of the oil, season and place the chicken on its side in a roasting tin. Put the remaining rosemary sprigs in the tin and drizzle the remaining oil around the tin.

Place the tin on the middle shelf in the oven. After 20 minutes, turn the chicken onto the other side, baste with the juices and cook for a further 20 minutes. Turn the chicken, breast side up, baste again and cook for a further 15 minutes, or until the juices between the body and thigh run clear when pierced with a knife. Transfer the chicken to a warm serving dish and set aside for at least 10 minutes before carving.

Meanwhile, pour off most of the fat from the roasting tin and return the tin to the stovetop over high heat. Add 2 tablespoons water and, using a wooden spoon, scrape the base of the pan to loosen the residue. Check the seasoning and pour over the chicken to serve.

Canja

❀ SERVES 6
❀ PREPARATION TIME: 15 MINUTES
❀ COOKING TIME: 1 HOUR

2.5 litres (88 fl oz/10 cups) chicken stock
1 onion, cut into thin wedges
1 celery stalk, finely chopped
1 teaspoon grated lemon zest
3 tomatoes, peeled, seeded and roughly
    chopped
1 mint sprig
1 tablespoon olive oil
2 boneless, skinless chicken breasts
200 g (7 oz/1 cup) long-grain rice
2 tablespoons lemon juice
2 tablespoons chopped mint

Combine the stock, onion, celery, lemon zest, tomato, mint and olive oil in a large saucepan. Slowly bring to the boil, then reduce the heat, add the chicken and simmer gently for 20–25 minutes, or until the chicken is cooked through.

Remove the chicken from the saucepan and discard the mint sprig. Allow the chicken to cool, then thinly slice.

Meanwhile, add the rice to the pan and simmer for 25–30 minutes, or until the rice is tender. Return the sliced chicken to the pan, add the lemon juice and stir for 1–2 minutes, or until the chicken is warmed through. Season to taste and stir in the chopped mint just before serving.

Herbed Poussins

❀ SERVES 4
❀ PREPARATION TIME: 30 MINUTES
❀ COOKING TIME: 35 MINUTES

125 g (4 oz) butter, softened
2 teaspoons chopped lemon thyme
1 tablespoon chopped flat-leaf (Italian)
    parsley
2 spring onions (scallions), finely chopped
1 teaspoon finely grated lemon zest
1 1/2 tablespoons lemon juice
4 x 500 g (1 lb 2 oz) poussins (baby
    chickens)
30 g (1 oz) butter, melted
2 teaspoons lemon juice, extra

Mix the softened butter with the herbs, spring onion, lemon zest, lemon juice, and plenty of salt and pepper.

Preheat the oven to 200°C (400°F/Gas 6). Cut the chickens down either side of the backbone. Discard the backbone, and gently flatten the chickens. Carefully lift the skin from the breastbone and the legs and push the herb butter underneath. Tuck in the wings and neck.

Place the chickens on a rack in a baking dish. Brush with the combined melted butter and extra lemon juice. Bake for 30–35 minutes, or until the juices run clear.

Canja

Hainanese Chicken Rice

✿ SERVES 6

✿ PREPARATION TIME: 50 MINUTES

✿ COOKING TIME: 1 HOUR 30 MINUTES

2 kg (4 lb 8 oz) chicken
6 spring onions (scallions), trimmed
a few thick slices fresh ginger
4 garlic cloves, bruised
1 teaspoon vegetable oil
1 teaspoon sesame oil

RICE
5 red Asian shallots or French shallots,
   finely chopped
2 garlic cloves, crushed
1 tablespoon very finely chopped
   fresh ginger
300 g (10½ oz/1½ cups) jasmine rice
100 g (3½ oz/½ cup) short-grain sticky
   (glutinous rice)
3 roma (plum) tomatoes, cut into thin
   wedges
3 Lebanese (short) cucumbers, sliced
   diagonally
coriander (cilantro) sprigs, to garnish

SAUCE
2 small red chillies, seeded and chopped
4 garlic cloves, roughly chopped
1½ tablespoons finely chopped
   fresh ginger
3 coriander (cilantro) roots, chopped
2 tablespoons dark soy sauce
2 tablespoons lime juice
2 tablespoons sugar
pinch ground white pepper

Remove the excess fat from around the cavity of the chicken and reserve. Rinse and salt the inside of the chicken and rinse again. Insert the spring onions, ginger slices and garlic into the chicken cavity, then place, breast side down, in a large saucepan and cover with cold water. Add 1 teaspoon salt and bring to the boil over high heat, skimming the surface as required. Reduce the heat to low and simmer gently for 15 minutes, then carefully turn over without piercing the skin and cook for another 15 minutes, or until the thigh juices run clear when pierced.

Carefully lift the chicken out of the saucepan, draining any liquid from the cavity into the rest of the stock. Reserve 1 litre (35 fl oz/4 cups) of the stock. Plunge the chicken into iced water for 5 minutes to stop the cooking process and to firm the skin. Rub the entire surface of the chicken with the combined vegetable and sesame oils and allow to cool while you make the rice.

To make the rice, cook the reserved chicken fat in a saucepan over medium heat for about 8 minutes, or until you have about 2 tablespoons of liquid fat, then discard the solids. Add the shallots and cook for a few minutes, or until lightly golden, then add the garlic and ginger and stir until fragrant. Add both the rices and cook for 5 minutes, or until golden, then pour in the reserved chicken stock and 1 teaspoon salt and bring to the boil. Cover, reduce the heat to low and cook for about 20 minutes, or until tender and the liquid has evaporated. Cool, covered, for 10 minutes, then fluff with a fork.

Meanwhile, to make the sauce, pound the chillies, garlic, ginger and coriander roots into a paste using a mortar and pestle. Stir in the rest of the ingredients and season to taste.

Shred the chicken. Divide the rice into six slightly wetted Chinese soup bowls and press down firmly, then turn out onto serving plates. Serve the pieces of chicken on a platter with the tomato, cucumber and coriander and pour the dipping sauce into a small bowl or individual sauce dishes and let your guests help themselves.

General Tso's Chicken

☆ SERVES 4–6
☆ PREPARATION TIME: 15 MINUTES
☆ COOKING TIME: 10 MINUTES

2 tablespoons Chinese rice wine
1 tablespoon cornflour (cornstarch)
80 ml (2½ fl oz/⅓ cup) dark soy sauce
3 teaspoons sesame oil
900 g (2 lb) boneless, skinless chicken
   thighs, cut into 3 cm (1¼ inch) cubes
2 pieces dried citrus peel
125 ml (4 fl oz/½ cup) peanut oil
1½–2 teaspoons chilli flakes
2 tablespoons finely chopped fresh ginger
65 g (2½ oz/1 cup) thinly sliced spring
   onions (scallions), plus extra, to
   garnish
2 teaspoons sugar
steamed rice, to serve

Combine the rice wine, cornflour, 2 tablespoons of the soy sauce and 2 teaspoons of the sesame oil in a large non-metallic bowl. Add the chicken, toss to coat in the marinade, then cover and marinate in the refrigerator for 1 hour.

Meanwhile, soak the dried citrus peel in warm water for 20 minutes. Remove from the water and finely chop — you will need 1½ teaspoons chopped peel.

Heat the peanut oil in a wok over high heat. Using a slotted spoon, drain the chicken from the marinade, then add to the wok in batches and stir-fry for 2 minutes at a time, or until browned and just cooked through. Remove from the oil with a slotted spoon and leave to drain in a colander or sieve.

Drain all the oil except 1 tablespoon from the wok. Reheat the wok over high heat, then add the chilli flakes and ginger. Stir-fry for 10 seconds, then return the chicken to the wok. Add the spring onion, sugar, chopped citrus peel, remaining soy sauce and sesame oil and ½ teaspoon salt and stir-fry for a further 2–3 minutes, or until well combined and warmed through. Garnish with the extra spring onion and serve with steamed rice.

NOTE: This dish is named after a 19th-century Chinese general from Yunnan province.

Chicken with Forty Cloves of Garlic

✤ SERVES 4
✤ PREPARATION TIME: 20 MINUTES
✤ COOKING TIME: 1 HOUR 40 MINUTES

10 g (¼ oz) butter
1 tablespoon olive oil
1 large chicken
40 garlic cloves, unpeeled
2 tablespoons chopped rosemary
2 thyme sprigs
270 ml (9½ fl oz) dry white wine
150 ml (5 fl oz) chicken stock
220 g (7¾ oz/1¾ cups) plain
    (all-purpose) flour

Preheat the oven to 180°C (350°F/Gas 4). Melt the butter and oil in a 4.5 litre (156 fl oz/18-cup) flameproof casserole dish, then brown the chicken over medium heat until golden all over. Remove the chicken and add the garlic, rosemary and thyme and cook together for 1 minute. Return the chicken to the dish and add the wine and chicken stock. Bring to a simmer, basting the chicken with the sauce.

Put the flour in a bowl and add up to 150 ml (5 fl oz) water to form a pliable paste. Divide into four and roll into cylinder shapes. Place around the rim of the casserole. Put the lid on the dish, pressing down to form a seal. Bake for 1¼ hours. Remove the lid by cracking the paste. Return the chicken to the oven to brown for 15 minutes, then transfer to a plate. Reduce the juices to 250 ml (9 fl oz/1 cup) over medium heat. Carve the chicken, pierce the garlic skins and squeeze the flesh onto the chicken. Serve with the sauce.

Chicken with Capsicum and Olives

✤ SERVES 4
✤ PREPARATION TIME: 30 MINUTES
✤ COOKING TIME: 1 HOUR 10 MINUTES

1.5 kg (3 lb 5 oz) chicken, cut into 8 portions
60 ml (2 fl oz/¼ cup) olive oil
2 large red onions, thinly sliced
2 garlic cloves, crushed
3 red capsicums (peppers), seeded and cut
    into 1 cm (½ inch) strips
60 g (2¼ oz) thickly sliced prosciutto,
    finely chopped
1 tablespoon chopped thyme
6 tomatoes, peeled, seeded and finely
    chopped
2 teaspoons sweet paprika
8 pitted black olives
8 pitted green olives

Pat the chicken dry with paper towels and season. Heat the oil in a heavy-based frying pan and cook the chicken a few pieces at a time, skin side down, for 4–5 minutes, until golden. Turn the chicken over and cook for another 2–3 minutes. Transfer to a plate.

Add the onion, garlic, capsicum, prosciutto and thyme to the pan. Cook over medium heat, stirring frequently for 8–10 minutes, or until the vegetables have softened but not browned. Add the tomato and paprika, increase the heat and cook for 10–12 minutes, or until the sauce has thickened and reduced. Return the chicken to the pan and coat well with the sauce. Cover the pan, reduce the heat and simmer the chicken for 25–30 minutes, or until tender. Add the olives and adjust the seasoning before serving.

Chicken with Forty Cloves of Garlic

Roast Turkey with Rice and Chestnut Stuffing

❄ SERVES 6–8

❄ PREPARATION TIME: 30 MINUTES

❄ COOKING TIME: 3 HOURS 30 MINUTES

STUFFING

12 prunes, pitted

185 g (6½ oz) whole fresh chestnuts

40 g (1½ oz) butter

1 red onion, finely chopped

2 garlic cloves, crushed

60 g (2¼ oz) pancetta (including any fat), finely chopped

105 g (3½ oz/½ cup) wild rice blend

60 ml (2 fl oz/¼ cup) chicken stock

3 dried juniper berries, lightly crushed

2 teaspoons finely chopped rosemary

3 teaspoons finely chopped thyme

3 kg (6 lb 12 oz) turkey, neck and giblets removed

1 large red onion, cut into 4–5 slices

30 g (1 oz) butter, softened

375 ml (13 fl oz/1½ cups) dry white wine

1 carrot, quartered

1 celery stalk, quartered

1 large rosemary sprig

2 teaspoons finely chopped thyme

250 ml (9 fl oz/1 cup) chicken stock

2 tablespoons plain (all-purpose) flour

Preheat the oven to 170°C (325°F/Gas 3). Soak the prunes in hot water for 20 minutes. Meanwhile, make a small cut in the skin on the flat side of each chestnut, put under a hot grill (broiler) and cook on both sides until well browned. Put the hot chestnuts in a bowl lined with a damp tea towel (dish towel) and cover with the towel. Leave until cool enough to handle, then peel. Roughly chop the prunes and chestnuts and set aside.

To make the stuffing, melt the butter in a large saucepan and add the onion, garlic and pancetta. Cook over low heat for 5–6 minutes, or until the onion is softened. Add the rice, stock, juniper berries, prunes and chestnuts, stir well, then pour in 375 ml (13 fl oz/1½ cups) water. Bring to the boil and cook, covered, stirring once or twice, for 20–25 minutes, or until the rice is tender and all liquid has been absorbed. Remove from the heat, stir in the rosemary and thyme, and season.

Wash and thoroughly pat dry the turkey. Fill the turkey cavity with the stuffing. Cross the turkey legs and tie them together, then tuck the wings underneath the body. Arrange the onion slices in the centre of a large roasting tin, then sit the turkey on top, breast side up. Season and dot with butter. Pour 250 ml (9 fl oz/1 cup) of the wine into the tin, then scatter the carrot, celery, rosemary and 1 teaspoon of the thyme around the turkey.

Roast for 2–2½ hours, or until cooked through and the juices run clear, basting every 30 minutes. After 1 hour, pour half the chicken stock into the tin. Once the skin becomes golden brown, cover with buttered foil.

When cooked, transfer the turkey to a carving plate, cover with foil and leave to rest in a warm spot. Meanwhile, pour the juices into a small saucepan and reduce for 8–10 minutes. Stir in the flour, then add the stock, a little at a time, stirring to form a paste. Slowly add the rest of the stock and wine, stirring so that no lumps form. Stir in the remaining thyme. Bring to the boil and simmer for 6–8 minutes, or until reduced by one-third, then season to taste. Transfer to a gravy boat. Carve the turkey and serve with the stuffing and gravy.

Chicken Chow Mein

❀ SERVES 4
❀ PREPARATION TIME: 15 MINUTES
❀ COOKING TIME: 40 MINUTES

250 g (9 oz) fresh thin egg noodles
2 teaspoons sesame oil
125 ml (4 fl oz/½ cup) peanut oil
1 tablespoon Chinese rice wine
1½ tablespoons light soy sauce
3 teaspoons cornflour (cornstarch)
400 g (14 oz) boneless, skinless chicken
    breasts, cut into thin strips
1 garlic clove, crushed
1 tablespoon finely chopped fresh ginger
100 g (3½ oz) sugar snap peas, trimmed
250 g (9 oz) Chinese cabbage (wong bok),
    finely shredded
4 spring onions (scallions), cut into 2 cm
    (¾ inch) lengths
100 ml (3½ fl oz) chicken stock
1½ tablespoons oyster sauce
100 g (3½ oz) bean sprouts
1 small red chilli, seeded and very thinly
    sliced, to garnish (optional)

Cook the noodles in a saucepan of boiling water for 1 minute, or until tender. Drain well. Add the sesame oil and 1 tablespoon of the peanut oil and toss well. Place on a baking tray and spread out in a thin layer. Leave in a dry place for at least 1 hour.

Meanwhile, combine the rice wine, 1 tablespoon soy sauce and 1 teaspoon cornflour in a large non-metallic bowl. Add the chicken and toss well to coat in the marinade. Cover with plastic wrap and marinate for 10 minutes.

Heat 1 tablespoon of the peanut oil in a small non-stick frying pan over high heat. Add one-quarter of the noodles, shaping them into a pancake. Reduce the heat to medium and cook for 4 minutes on each side, or until crisp and golden. Drain on crumpled paper towel and keep warm. Repeat with 3 tablespoons of the oil and the remaining noodles to make four noodle cakes in total.

Heat a wok over high heat, add the remaining peanut oil and swirl to coat the base and side. Stir-fry the garlic and ginger for 30 seconds, then add the chicken and stir-fry for 3–4 minutes, or until golden and tender. Add the sugar snap peas, Chinese cabbage and spring onion and stir-fry for 2 minutes, or until the cabbage has wilted. Stir in the stock, oyster sauce and bean sprouts and bring to the boil.

Combine the remaining cornflour with 1–2 teaspoons cold water. Stir the cornflour mixture into the wok along with the remaining soy sauce and cook for 1–2 minutes, or until the sauce thickens.

To assemble, place a noodle cake on each serving plate and then spoon the chicken and vegetable mixture on top. Serve immediately, garnished with chilli, if desired.

Chicken Pie with Feta

⚜ SERVES 6
⚜ PREPARATION TIME: 30 MINUTES
⚜ COOKING TIME: 1 HOUR 10 MINUTES

1 kg (2 lb 4 oz) boneless, skinless chicken
    breast
500 ml (17 fl oz/2 cups) chicken stock
60 g (2¼ oz) butter
2 spring onions (scallions), finely chopped
60 g (2¼ oz/½ cup) plain (all-purpose)
    flour
125 ml (4 fl oz/½ cup) milk
8 sheets filo pastry (30 x 40 cm/
    12 x 16 inches)
60 g (2¼ oz) butter, extra, melted
200 g (7 oz) feta, crumbled
1 tablespoon chopped dill
1 tablespoon snipped chives
¼ teaspoon freshly grated nutmeg
1 egg, lightly beaten

Cut the chicken into bite-sized pieces. Pour the stock into a saucepan and bring to the boil over high heat. Reduce the heat to low, add the chicken and poach gently for 10–15 minutes, or until the chicken is cooked through. Drain, reserving the stock. Add enough water to the stock in order to bring the quantity up to 500 ml (17 fl oz/2 cups). Preheat the oven to 180°C (350°F/Gas 4).

Melt the butter in a saucepan over low heat, add the spring onion and cook, stirring, for 5 minutes. Add the flour and stir for 30 seconds. Remove the pan from the heat and gradually add the chicken stock and milk, stirring after each addition. Return to the heat and gently bring to the boil, stirring. Simmer for a few minutes, or until the sauce thickens. Remove from the heat.

Line an ovenproof dish measuring 4 x 18 x 25 cm (1½ x 7 x 10 inches) with four sheets of filo pastry, brushing one side of each sheet with the melted butter as you go. Place the buttered side down. The filo will overlap the edges of the dish. Cover the unused filo with a damp tea towel (dish towel) to prevent it drying out.

Stir the chicken, feta, dill, chives, nutmeg and egg into the sauce, then season to taste. Pile the mixture on top of the filo pastry in the dish. Fold the overlapping filo over the filling and cover the top of the pie with the remaining four sheets of filo, brushing each sheet with melted butter as you go. Scrunch the edges of the pastry so that they fit in the dish. Brush the top with butter. Bake for 45–50 minutes, or until the pastry is golden brown and crisp.

NOTE: If you prefer, you can use puff pastry instead of filo pastry. If you do so, bake in a 220°C (425°F/Gas 7) oven for 15 minutes, then reduce the temperature to 180°C (350°F/Gas 4) and cook for another 30 minutes, or until the pastry is golden.

Roast Duck with Olives

SAUCE
1 tablespoon olive oil
1 onion, chopped
1 garlic clove, crushed
2 ripe roma (plum) tomatoes, peeled,
     seeded and finely chopped
250 ml (9 fl oz/1 cup) Riesling
2 teaspoons thyme
1 bay leaf
24 niçoise olives, pitted

STUFFING
60 g (2¼ oz/⅓ cup) medium-grain white
     rice, cooked
1 garlic clove, crushed
100 g (3½ oz) frozen chopped spinach,
     defrosted
2 ducks' livers (about 100 g/3½ oz),
     chopped
1 egg, lightly beaten
1 teaspoon thyme

1.8 kg (4 lb) duck
2 bay leaves

Preheat the oven to 200°C (400°F/Gas 6). To make the sauce, heat the oil in a frying pan, add the onion and cook for 5 minutes, or until transparent. Add the garlic, tomato, wine and herbs and season. Cook for 5 minutes, then add the olives before removing from the heat.

To make the stuffing, thoroughly mix all the ingredients in a bowl and season well. Before stuffing the duck, rinse out the cavity with cold water and pat dry inside and out with paper towels. Put the bay leaves in the cavity, then spoon in the stuffing.

Tuck the wings under the duck, then close the flaps of fat over the parson's nose and secure with a skewer or toothpick. Place in a deep roasting tin and rub 1 teaspoon salt into the skin. Prick the skin all over with a skewer.

Roast on the top shelf of the oven for 35–40 minutes, then carefully pour off the excess fat. Roast for another 35–40 minutes. To check that the duck is cooked, gently pull away one leg from the side. The flesh should be pale brown with no blood in the juices. Carve the duck, then serve with a spoonful of the stuffing and top with the sauce.

Chicken Laksa

1 1/2 tablespoons coriander seeds

1 tablespoon cumin seeds

1 teaspoon ground turmeric

1 onion, roughly chopped

1 tablespoon roughly chopped ginger

3 garlic cloves

3 lemongrass stems, white part only, sliced

6 macadamia nuts

4–6 small red chillies

3 teaspoons shrimp paste, roasted
   (see Note)

1 litre (35 fl oz/4 cups) chicken stock

60 ml (2 fl oz/1/4 cup) vegetable oil

400 g (14 oz) boneless, skinless chicken
   thigh, cut into 2 cm (3/4 inch) pieces

750 ml (26 fl oz/3 cups) coconut milk

4 kaffir lime leaves

2 1/2 tablespoons lime juice

2 tablespoons fish sauce

2 tablespoons grated palm sugar (jaggery)
   or soft brown sugar

250 g (9 oz) dried rice vermicelli

90 g (3 1/4 oz/1 cup) bean sprouts,
   trimmed

4 fried tofu puffs, cut into thin batons

3 tablespoons chopped Vietnamese mint

1 handful coriander (cilantro) leaves

lime wedges, to serve

Toast the coriander and cumin seeds in a frying pan over medium heat for 1–2 minutes, or until fragrant, tossing the pan constantly to prevent them from burning. Grind finely using a mortar and pestle or a spice grinder.

Put all the spices, onion, ginger, garlic, lemongrass, macadamia nuts, chillies and shrimp paste in a food processor or blender. Add 125 ml (4 fl oz/1/2 cup) of the stock and blend to a paste.

Heat the oil in a wok or large saucepan over low heat and gently cook the paste for 3–5 minutes, stirring constantly to prevent it burning or sticking to the bottom of the pan. Add the remaining stock and bring to the boil over high heat. Reduce the heat to medium and simmer for 15 minutes, or until reduced slightly. Add the chicken and simmer for 4–5 minutes. Add the coconut milk, kaffir lime leaves, lime juice, fish sauce and palm sugar and simmer for 5 minutes over medium–low heat. Do not bring to the boil or cover with a lid, as the coconut milk will split.

Meanwhile, put the vermicelli in a heatproof bowl, cover with boiling water and soak for 6–7 minutes, or until softened. Drain and divide among large serving bowls with the bean sprouts. Ladle the hot soup over the top and garnish with some tofu strips, mint and coriander leaves. Serve with wedges of lime.

NOTE: To roast the shrimp paste, wrap the paste in foil and put under a hot grill (broiler) for 1 minute.

Chicken Cacciatora

❧ SERVES 4

❧ PREPARATION TIME: 15 MINUTES

❧ COOKING TIME: 1 HOUR

60 ml (2 fl oz/¼ cup) olive oil

1 large onion, finely chopped

3 garlic cloves, crushed

150 g (5½ oz) pancetta, finely chopped

125 g (4½ oz) button mushrooms, thickly
  sliced

1 large chicken (at least 1.6 kg/3 lb 8 oz),
  cut into 8 pieces

80 ml (2½ fl oz/⅓ cup) dry vermouth or
  dry white wine

800 g (1 lb 12 oz) tinned chopped
  tomatoes

¼ teaspoon soft brown sugar

¼ teaspoon cayenne pepper

1 oregano sprig

1 thyme sprig

1 bay leaf

Heat half the oil in a large flameproof casserole dish. Add the onion and garlic and cook, over low heat, for 6–8 minutes, stirring, until the onion is golden. Add the pancetta and mushrooms, increase the heat and cook, stirring, for 4–5 minutes. Transfer to a bowl.

Add the remaining oil to the casserole dish and brown the chicken pieces, a few at a time, over medium heat. Season as they brown. Spoon off the excess fat and return all the chicken to the casserole dish. Increase the heat, add the vermouth or wine to the dish and cook until the liquid has almost evaporated.

Add the chopped tomato, brown sugar, cayenne pepper, oregano, thyme and bay leaf, and stir in 80 ml (2½ fl oz/⅓ cup) water. Bring to the boil, then stir in the reserved onion mixture. Reduce the heat, cover and simmer for 25 minutes, or until the chicken is tender but not falling off the bone.

If the liquid is too thin, remove the chicken from the casserole dish, increase the heat and boil until the liquid has thickened. Discard the sprigs of herbs and adjust the seasoning.

Chicken, Thai Basil and Cashew Stir-Fry

※ SERVES 4
※ PREPARATION TIME: 15 MINUTES
※ COOKING TIME: 10 MINUTES

750 g (1 lb 10 oz) boneless, skinless
    chicken breast, cut into strips
2 lemongrass stems, white part only, finely
    chopped
3 small red chillies, seeded and chopped
4 garlic cloves, crushed
1 tablespoon finely chopped fresh ginger
2 coriander (cilantro) roots, chopped
2 tablespoons vegetable oil
100 g (3½ oz/⅔ cup) cashew nuts
1½ tablespoons lime juice
2 tablespoons fish sauce
1½ tablespoons grated palm sugar
    (jaggery) or soft brown sugar
2 very large handfuls Thai basil
2 teaspoons cornflour (cornstarch)

Put the chicken in a large bowl with the lemongrass, chilli, garlic, ginger and coriander root. Mix well.

Heat a wok over medium heat, add 1 teaspoon of the oil and swirl to coat. Add the cashews and cook for 1 minute, or until lightly golden. Remove and drain on crumpled paper towels.

Heat the remaining oil in the wok, add the chicken in batches and stir-fry over medium heat for 4–5 minutes, or until browned. Return the chicken to the wok.

Stir in the lime juice, fish sauce, palm sugar and basil, and cook for 30–60 seconds, or until the basil just begins to wilt. Mix the cornflour with 1 tablespoon water, add to the wok and stir until the mixture thickens slightly. Stir in the cashews and serve with steamed rice.

Chicken Braised with Ginger and Star Anise

※ SERVES 4
※ PREPARATION TIME: 10 MINUTES
※ COOKING TIME: 30 MINUTES

1 teaspoon sichuan peppercorns
2 tablespoons peanut oil
2 x 3 cm (¾ x 1¼ inch) piece fresh
    ginger, cut into thin batons
2 garlic cloves, chopped
1 kg (2 lb 4 oz) boneless, skinless chicken
    thighs, halved
80 ml (2½ fl oz/⅓ cup) Chinese rice
    wine
1 tablespoon honey
60 ml (2 fl oz/¼ cup) light soy sauce
1 star anise

Heat a wok over medium heat, add the peppercorns and cook, stirring often, for 2–4 minutes, or until fragrant. Remove and lightly crush with the back of a knife.

Reheat the wok, add the oil and swirl to coat. Add the ginger and garlic and cook over low heat for 1–2 minutes, or until lightly golden. Add the chicken, increase the heat to medium and cook for 3 minutes, or until browned all over.

Add the remaining ingredients, reduce the heat and simmer, covered, for 20 minutes, or until the chicken is tender. Serve with steamed rice.

Chicken, Thai Basil and Cashew Stir-Fry

Turkey Roll with Mandarin Sauce

⚜ SERVES 8
⚜ PREPARATION TIME: 1 HOUR
⚜ COOKING TIME: 2 HOURS

90 g (3¼ oz) dried apricots, chopped
30 g (1 oz) butter
1 onion, finely chopped
1 garlic clove, crushed
400 g (14 oz) minced (ground) chicken
120 g (4 oz/1½ cups) fresh breadcrumbs
35 g (1¼ oz/½ cup) currants
35 g (1¼ oz/¼ cup) pistachio nuts,
    toasted and chopped
3 tablespoons chopped flat-leaf (Italian)
    parsley
3.4 kg (7 lb 13 oz) turkey, boned
olive oil, for rubbing

MANDARIN SAUCE
2 mandarins
1 tablespoon long thin strips of mandarin
    zest
2 tablespoons sugar
1 tablespoon brandy
250 ml (9 fl oz/1 cup) mandarin juice
80 ml (2½ fl oz/⅓ cup) chicken stock
3 teaspoons cornflour (cornstarch)
1 spring onion (scallion), finely sliced

Place the apricots in a small bowl, cover with boiling water and soak for 30 minutes. Preheat the oven to 180°C (350°F/Gas 4).

Meanwhile, melt the butter in a frying pan, add the onion and garlic and cook, stirring, for about 5 minutes, or until the onion is soft. Remove from the heat. Combine the mince, onion mixture, breadcrumbs, currants, nuts, parsley and apricots in a bowl and mix well. Season. Place the turkey on the work surface, skin side down and form the stuffing mixture into a large sausage shape about the same length as the turkey. Fold the turkey over to enclose the stuffing. Secure with toothpicks or skewers and truss with kitchen string at 3 cm (1¼ inch) intervals.

Place on a lightly greased baking tray. Rub with a little oil and season. Roast the turkey roll for 1½–2 hours, or until the juices run clear. Cover and set aside for 10 minutes while preparing the sauce. Carefully remove the string and toothpicks. Cut into slices and serve with the mandarin sauce.

To make the mandarin sauce, segment the mandarins. Remove the zest and white pith, then cut between the membranes to release the segments. Place the zest in a saucepan, cover with water and bring to the boil. Drain and repeat. Sprinkle the sugar over the base of a saucepan over medium heat and stir until all the sugar has dissolved. Remove from the heat, cool, then stir in the brandy. Return to the heat, stir to dissolve any toffee, then add the combined mandarin juice and chicken stock. Add the combined cornflour and 1 tablespoon water and stir over heat until the mixture thickens. Add the mandarin segments and zest, stirring until heated through. Stir in the spring onion, then season.

Mild Vietnamese Chicken Curry

※ SERVES 6
※ PREPARATION TIME: 30 MINUTES
※ COOKING TIME: 1 HOUR 10 MINUTES

125 g (4½ oz) dried rice vermicelli
185 ml (6 fl oz/¾ cup) vegetable oil
4 large chicken quarters (leg and thigh),
   skin and excess fat removed, cut into
   thirds
1 tablespoon curry powder
1 teaspoon caster (superfine) sugar
80 ml (2½ fl oz/⅓ cup) vegetable oil,
   extra
500 g (1 lb 2 oz) orange sweet potato,
   peeled, cut into 3 cm (1¼ inch) cubes
1 large onion, cut into thin wedges
4 garlic cloves, chopped
1 lemongrass stem, white part only, finely
   chopped
2 bay leaves
1 large carrot, cut diagonally into 1 cm
   (½ inch) pieces
400 ml (14 fl oz) coconut milk

Break the vermicelli into short lengths. Heat half the oil in a wok over medium heat. Cook the vermicelli in batches until crisp, adding more oil when necessary. Drain on paper towel and set aside.

Pat the chicken dry with paper towel. Put the curry powder, sugar, ½ teaspoon black pepper and 2 teaspoons salt in a bowl, and mix together well. Rub the curry mixture onto the chicken pieces then place the chicken on a plate, cover with plastic wrap and refrigerate overnight.

Heat a wok over high heat, add the oil and swirl to coat the base and side. Add the sweet potato and cook over medium heat for 3 minutes, or until lightly golden. Remove with a slotted spoon and set aside.

Remove all but 2 tablespoons of the oil from the wok. Add the onion and cook, stirring, for 5 minutes. Add the garlic, lemongrass and bay leaves, and cook for 2 minutes. Add the chicken and cook, stirring, over medium heat for 5 minutes, or until well coated in the mixture and starting to change colour.

Add 250 ml (9 fl oz/1 cup) water and simmer, covered, over low heat for 20 minutes, stirring occasionally. Add the carrot, sweet potato and coconut milk, and simmer, uncovered, stirring occasionally, for 30 minutes, or until the chicken is cooked and tender. Be careful not to break up the sweet potato cubes. Serve with the crisp vermicelli.

Cantonese Lemon Chicken

❄ SERVES 4

❄ PREPARATION TIME: 15 MINUTES

❄ COOKING TIME: 25 MINUTES

500 g (1 lb 2 oz) boneless, skinless
   chicken breasts
1 egg yolk, lightly beaten
2 teaspoons soy sauce
2 teaspoons dry sherry
3 teaspoons cornflour (cornstarch)
60 g (2¼ oz/½ cup) cornflour
   (cornstarch), extra
2½ tablespoons plain (all-purpose) flour
vegetable oil, for deep-frying
4 spring onions (scallions), thinly sliced

LEMON SAUCE
80 ml (2½ fl oz/⅓ cup) lemon juice
2 tablespoons sugar
1 tablespoon dry sherry
2 teaspoons cornflour (cornstarch)

Cut the chicken into long strips, about 1 cm (½ inch) wide, and then set aside. Combine the egg, 1 tablespoon water, soy sauce, sherry and cornflour in a small bowl and mix until smooth. Pour the egg mixture over the chicken, mixing well, and set aside for 10 minutes.

Sift the extra cornflour and plain flour together onto a plate. Roll each piece of chicken in the flour, coating each piece evenly, and shake off the excess. Place the chicken in a single layer on a plate.

Fill a wok one-third full of oil and heat to 180°C (350°F), or until a cube of bread dropped into the oil browns in 15 seconds. Carefully lower the chicken pieces into the oil, in batches, and cook for 2 minutes, or until golden brown. Remove the chicken with a slotted spoon and drain on paper towel. Repeat with the remaining chicken. Set aside while preparing the sauce. Reserve the oil in the wok.

To make the lemon sauce, combine 2 tablespoons water, the lemon juice, sugar and sherry in a small saucepan. Bring to the boil over medium heat, stirring until the sugar dissolves. Stir the cornflour into 1 tablespoon water and mix to a smooth paste, then add to the lemon juice mixture, stirring constantly until the sauce boils and thickens. Set aside.

Just before serving, reheat the oil in the wok to very hot, add all the chicken pieces and deep-fry for 2 minutes, or until very crisp and a rich golden brown. Remove the chicken with a slotted spoon and drain well on paper towel. Pile the chicken onto a serving plate, drizzle over the sauce, sprinkle with spring onion and serve immediately.

NOTE: The first deep-frying of the chicken pieces can be done several hours in advance.

Tandoori Chicken with Cardamom Rice

❧ SERVES 4
❧ PREPARATION TIME: 15 MINUTES
❧ COOKING TIME: 45 MINUTES

250 g (9 oz/1 cup) Greek-style yoghurt
60 g (2¼ oz/¼ cup) tandoori paste
    (see Note)
2 tablespoons lemon juice
1 kg (2 lb 4 oz) boneless, skinless chicken
    breasts, cut into 4 cm (1½ inch) cubes
1 tablespoon vegetable oil
1 onion, finely diced
300 g (10½ oz/1½ cups) long-grain rice
2 cardamom pods, bruised
750 ml (26 fl oz/3 cups) hot chicken stock
400 g (14 oz) baby English spinach leaves
Greek-style yoghurt, extra, to serve

Soak eight bamboo skewers in water for 30 minutes to prevent them burning during cooking.

Meanwhile, combine the yoghurt, tandoori paste and lemon juice in a non-metallic dish. Add the chicken and coat well, then cover with plastic wrap and marinate for at least 10 minutes.

Heat the oil in a saucepan, add the onion and cook for 3 minutes, then add the rice and cardamom pods. Cook, stirring often, for 3–5 minutes, or until the rice is slightly opaque. Add the hot stock and bring to the boil. Reduce the heat to low, then cover and cook the rice, without removing the lid, for 15 minutes.

Meanwhile, wash the spinach and put it in a large saucepan with just the water clinging to the leaves. Cook, covered, over medium heat for 1–2 minutes, or until the spinach has wilted. Set aside and keep warm.

Preheat a barbecue plate or grill (broiler) to very hot. Thread the chicken cubes onto the soaked bamboo skewers, leaving the bottom quarter of the skewers empty. Cook the skewers on each side for 4–5 minutes, or until the chicken is cooked through.

Uncover the rice, fluff up with a fork and serve with the spinach, chicken and a dollop of extra yoghurt.

NOTE: Tandoori paste is usually made up of a mixture of cumin, ground coriander, cinnamon, cloves, chilli, ginger, garlic, turmeric, mace, salt, colouring and yoghurt, though recipes do vary. There are many commercial varieties of paste available in jars from Indian grocery stores and large supermarkets.

Chicken and Almond Pilaff

※ SERVES 4–6
※ PREPARATION TIME: 15 MINUTES
※ COOKING TIME: 45 MINUTES

BAHARAT

1 1/2 tablespoons coriander seeds
3 tablespoons black peppercorns
1 1/2 tablespoons cassia bark
1 1/2 tablespoons whole cloves
2 tablespoons cumin seeds
1 teaspoon cardamom seeds
2 whole nutmegs
3 tablespoons paprika

700 g (1 lb 9 oz) boneless, skinless
   chicken thighs, trimmed and cut into
   3 cm (1 1/4 inch) wide strips
400 g (14 oz/2 cups) basmati rice
750 ml (26 fl oz/3 cups) chicken stock
2 tablespoons ghee
1 large onion, chopped
1 garlic clove, finely chopped
1 teaspoon ground turmeric
400 g (14 oz) tinned chopped tomatoes
1 cinnamon stick
4 cardamom pods, bruised
4 whole cloves
1/2 teaspoon finely grated lemon zest
3 tablespoons chopped coriander (cilantro)
   leaves
2 teaspoons lemon juice
40 g (1 1/2 oz/1/3 cup) slivered almonds,
   toasted

To make the baharat, grind the coriander seeds, peppercorns, cassia bark, cloves, cumin seeds and cardamom seeds to a powder using a mortar and pestle or a spice grinder — you may need to do this in batches. Grate the nutmeg on the fine side of the grater and add to the spice mixture with the paprika. Stir together.

Combine the chicken and 1 tablespoon of the baharat in a large bowl, cover with plastic wrap and refrigerate for 1 hour. Meanwhile, put the rice in a large bowl, cover with cold water and soak for at least 30 minutes. Rinse under cold, running water until the water runs clear, then drain and set aside.

Bring the stock to the boil in a saucepan. Reduce the heat, cover and keep at a low simmer. Meanwhile, heat the ghee in a large, heavy-based saucepan over medium heat. Add the onion and garlic and cook for 5 minutes, or until soft and golden. Add the chicken and turmeric and cook for 5 minutes, or until browned. Add the rice and cook, stirring, for 2 minutes.

Add the tomato, simmering chicken stock, cinnamon stick, cardamom pods, cloves, lemon zest and 1 teaspoon salt. Stir well and bring to the boil, then reduce the heat to low and cover the saucepan with a tight-fitting lid. Simmer for 20 minutes, or until the stock is absorbed and the rice is cooked. Remove from the heat and allow to stand, covered, for 10 minutes.

Stir in the coriander, lemon juice and almonds. Season to taste.

NOTE: Baharat is an aromatic spice blend used in Arabic cuisine to add depth of flavour to dishes such as soups, fish curries and tomato sauces. Baharat can be stored in an airtight jar for up to 3 months in a cool, dry place. It can be used in Middle Eastern casseroles and warming winter stews, rubbed on fish that is to be grilled (broiled), pan-fried or barbecued, or used with salt as a spice rub for lamb roasts, cutlets or chops.

Curry Mee Noodles

2 large dried red chillies
1 teaspoon shrimp paste
400 g (14 oz) hokkien (egg) noodles
1 onion, chopped
4 garlic cloves, chopped
4 lemongrass stems, white part only, thinly
   sliced
1 teaspoon grated fresh ginger
500 ml (17 fl oz/2 cups) coconut cream
30 g (1 oz/¼ cup) Malaysian curry
   powder
400 g (14 oz) boneless, skinless chicken
   thighs, thinly sliced
120 g (4¼ oz) green beans, trimmed and
   cut into 5 cm (2 inch) lengths
750 ml (26 fl oz/3 cups) chicken stock
10 fried tofu puffs, halved diagonally
2 tablespoons fish sauce
2 teaspoons sugar
180 g (6¼ oz/2 cups) bean sprouts
2 hard-boiled eggs, quartered
2 tablespoons crisp-fried shallots
lime wedges, to serve

Soak the chillies in boiling water for 20 minutes. Drain, then chop. Wrap the shrimp paste in foil and put under a hot grill (broiler) for 1–2 minutes. Unwrap the shrimp paste.

Put the noodles in a bowl, cover with boiling water and soak for 1 minute to separate. Rinse under cold water, drain and set aside.

Put the onion, garlic, lemongrass, ginger, chilli and shrimp paste in a food processor or blender and process to a rough paste, adding a little water if necessary.

Put 250 ml (9 fl oz/1 cup) of the coconut cream in a wok and bring to the boil, then simmer for 10 minutes, or until the oil starts to separate from the cream. Stir in the paste and curry powder and cook for 5 minutes, or until fragrant. Add the chicken and beans and cook for 3–4 minutes, or until the chicken is almost cooked. Add the stock, tofu puffs, fish sauce, sugar and the remaining coconut cream. Simmer, covered, over low heat for 10 minutes, or until the chicken is cooked.

Divide the noodles and bean sprouts among four bowls, then ladle the curry over the top. Garnish with the egg quarters and crisp fried shallots. Serve with the lime wedges.

Chicken Kapitan

* SERVES 4–6
* PREPARATION TIME: 35 MINUTES
* COOKING TIME: 30 MINUTES

30 g (1 oz) small dried shrimp
80 ml (2½ fl oz/⅓ cup) vegetable oil
4–8 red chillies, seeded and finely chopped
4 garlic cloves, finely chopped
3 lemongrass stems (white part only),
    finely chopped
2 teaspoons ground turmeric
10 candlenuts or macadamia nutes
2 large onions, chopped
250 ml (9 fl oz/1 cup) coconut milk
500 g (1 lb 2 oz) boneless, skinless
    chicken thighs, chopped
125 ml (4 fl oz/½ cup) coconut cream
2 tablespoons lime juice
steamed rice, to serve

Put the shrimp in a frying pan and dry-fry over low heat, shaking the pan regularly, for 3 minutes, or until the shrimp are dark orange and are giving off a strong aroma. Transfer the shrimp to a mortar and pestle and pound until finely ground. Set aside.

Put half the oil with the chilli, garlic, lemongrass, turmeric and candlenuts in a food processor and process in short bursts until very finely chopped, regularly scraping down the sides of the bowl with a rubber spatula.

Heat the remaining oil in a wok or frying pan, add the onion and ¼ teaspoon salt and cook over low heat for 8 minutes, or until golden, stirring regularly. Take care not to let the onion burn. Add the spice mixture and nearly all the ground shrimp, setting a little aside to use as garnish. Stir for 5 minutes. If the mixture begins to stick to the bottom of the pan, add 2 tablespoons coconut milk to the mixture. It is important to cook the mixture thoroughly to develop the flavours.

Add the chicken to the wok and stir well. Cook for 5 minutes, or until the chicken begins to brown. Stir in the remaining coconut milk and 250 ml (9 fl oz/1 cup) water, and bring to the boil. Reduce the heat and simmer for 7 minutes, or until the chicken is cooked and the sauce is thick. Add the coconut cream and bring the mixture back to the boil, stirring constantly. Add the lime juice and serve immediately, sprinkled lightly with the reserved ground shrimp. Serve with steamed rice.

Chicken with Almonds and Asparagus

※ SERVES 4–6
※ PREPARATION TIME: 15 MINUTES
※ COOKING TIME: 15 MINUTES

2 teaspoons cornflour (cornstarch)
80 ml (2½ fl oz/⅓ cup) chicken stock
¼ teaspoon sesame oil
2 tablespoons oyster sauce
1 tablespoon soy sauce
3 garlic cloves, crushed
1 teaspoon finely chopped fresh ginger
pinch ground white pepper
2½ tablespoons peanut oil
50 g (1¾ oz/⅓ cup) blanched almonds
2 spring onions (scallions), cut into 3 cm
    (1¼ inch) lengths
500 g (1 lb 2 oz) boneless, skinless
    chicken thighs, cut into thin strips
1 small carrot, thinly sliced
155 g (5½ oz) asparagus, trimmed and
    cut into 3 cm (1¼ inch) lengths
60 g (2¼ oz/¼ cup) tinned bamboo
    shoots, sliced
steamed rice, to serve

To make the stir-fry sauce, put the cornflour and stock in a small bowl and mix to form a paste, then stir in the sesame oil, oyster sauce, soy sauce, garlic, ginger and white pepper. Set aside until needed.

Heat a wok over high heat, add 2 teaspoons of the peanut oil and swirl to coat the base and side. Add the almonds and stir-fry for 1–2 minutes, or until golden — be careful not to burn them. Remove from the wok and drain on crumpled paper towel.

Heat another teaspoon of the peanut oil in the wok and swirl to coat. Add the spring onion and stir-fry for 30 seconds, or until wilted. Remove from the wok and set aside.

Heat 1 tablespoon of the peanut oil in the wok over high heat, add the chicken in two batches and stir-fry for 3 minutes, or until the chicken is just cooked through. Set aside with the spring onion.

Add the remaining peanut oil to the wok, then add the carrot and stir-fry for 1–2 minutes, or until just starting to brown. Toss in the asparagus and the bamboo shoots and stir-fry for a further 1 minute. Remove all the vegetables from the wok and set aside with the chicken and spring onion.

Stir the stir-fry sauce briefly, then pour into the wok, stirring until the mixture thickens. Return the chicken and vegetables to the wok and stir thoroughly for a couple of minutes until they are coated in the sauce and are heated through. Transfer to a serving dish and sprinkle with the almonds before serving. Serve with steamed rice.

Roast Chicken with Bacon and Sage Stuffing

❀ SERVES 6
❀ PREPARATION TIME: 15 MINUTES
❀ COOKING TIME: 1 HOUR 10 MINUTES

2 x 1.2 kg (2 lb 12 oz) chickens
6 bacon slices
2 tablespoons olive oil
1 small onion, finely chopped
1 tablespoon chopped sage
120 g (4¼ oz/1½ cups) fresh
    breadcrumbs
1 egg, lightly beaten

WINE GRAVY
2 tablespoons plain (all-purpose) flour
2 teaspoons worcestershire sauce
2 tablespoons red or white wine
560 ml (19¼ fl oz/2¼ cups) beef or
    chicken stock

Preheat the oven to 180°C (350°F/Gas 4). Remove the giblets and any large fat deposits from the chickens. Wipe over and pat dry inside and out with paper towels.

Finely chop two of the bacon slices. Heat half the oil in a small frying pan. Add the onion and the finely chopped bacon and cook until the onion is soft and the bacon is starting to brown. Transfer to a bowl and cool. Add the sage, breadcrumbs and egg to the onion, season, to taste, and mix lightly. Spoon some stuffing into each chicken cavity.

Fold the wings back and tuck under the chickens. Tie the legs of each chicken together with string. Place the chickens on a rack in a large baking dish, making sure they are not touching, and brush with some of the remaining oil. Pour 250 ml (9 fl oz/1 cup) water into the baking dish.

Cut the remaining bacon into long, thin strips and lay across the chicken breasts. Brush the bacon with oil. Bake for 45–60 minutes, or until the juices run clear when a thigh is pierced with a skewer.

To make the gravy, discard all but 2 tablespoons of the pan juices from the baking dish you cooked the chickens in. Heat the dish on the stovetop over medium heat, stir in the flour and cook, stirring, until well browned. Remove from the heat and gradually add the worcestershire sauce, wine and stock. Return to the heat, stir until the mixture boils and thickens, then simmer for 2 minutes. Season with salt and pepper, to taste.

Thai Green Chicken Curry

❀ SERVES 4
❀ PREPARATION TIME: 15 MINUTES
❀ COOKING TIME: 30 MINUTES

CURRY PASTE

1 tablespoon shrimp paste
1 teaspoon coriander seeds, toasted
$1/2$ teaspoon cumin seeds, toasted
$1/4$ teaspoon white peppercorns
5 coriander (cilantro) roots
3 tablespoons chopped fresh galangal
10 long green chillies, chopped
1 lemongrass stem, white part only,
    chopped
6 red Asian shallots or French shallots
3 garlic cloves
1 teaspoon grated lime zest
2 tablespoons peanut oil

250 ml (9 fl oz/1 cup) coconut cream
500 g (1 lb 2 oz) boneless, skinless
    chicken thighs, thinly sliced
125 g ($4^1/2$ oz) snake (yard-long) beans,
    sliced
500 ml (17 fl oz/2 cups) coconut milk
150 g ($5^1/2$ oz) broccoli, cut into small
    florets
1 tablespoon grated palm sugar (jaggery)
    or soft brown sugar
2–3 tablespoons fish sauce
5 tablespoons coriander (cilantro) leaves,
    plus extra, to garnish
steamed rice, to serve

To make the curry paste, preheat the grill (broiler) to high, wrap the shrimp paste in foil, and put under the hot grill for 5 minutes. Cool, remove the foil then put the shrimp paste in a food processor.

Put the coriander seeds, cumin seeds and peppercorns in a mortar and pestle and grind to a fine powder. Transfer to the food processor with $1/4$ teaspoon salt and the remaining paste ingredients. Blend until smooth.

Put the coconut cream in a wok over high heat, bring to the boil, then simmer for 10 minutes, or until the oil starts to separate from the cream. Reduce the heat to medium. Stir in half the curry paste and cook for 2–3 minutes, or until fragrant. Add the chicken and cook for 3–4 minutes. Stir in the beans, coconut milk and broccoli. Bring to the boil then reduce the heat and simmer for 4–5 minutes, or until cooked. Stir in the palm sugar, fish sauce and coriander leaves. Garnish with the extra coriander and serve with steamed rice.

NOTE: Store the remaining curry paste in an airtight container in the refrigerator for up to 2 weeks.

Barbecued Chicken with Thai Sticky Rice

❀ SERVES 4–6
❀ PREPARATION TIME: 30 MINUTES
❀ COOKING TIME: 1 HOUR

2 kg (4 lb 8 oz) chicken, cut into
    8–10 pieces
8 garlic cloves, chopped
6 coriander (cilantro) roots, chopped
1 large handful coriander (cilantro) leaves,
    chopped
1 tablespoon finely chopped fresh ginger
1 teaspoon ground white pepper
60 ml (2 fl oz/¼ cup) fish sauce
60 ml (2 fl oz/¼ cup) lime juice
60 ml (2 fl oz/¼ cup) whisky (optional)
600 g (1 lb 5 oz/3 cups) short-grain
    sticky (glutinous) rice
cucumber slices, to serve

SAUCE
6 coriander (cilantro) roots, chopped
4 garlic cloves, chopped
2 bird's eye chillies, seeded and chopped
185 ml (6 fl oz/¾ cup) vinegar
4 tablespoons grated palm sugar (jaggery)
    or soft brown sugar

Put the chicken pieces in a non-metallic bowl. Combine the garlic, coriander root and leaves, ginger, white pepper and a pinch of salt and pound to a paste using a mortar and pestle. Mix in the fish sauce, lime juice and whisky (if desired), then pour over the chicken and mix well. Marinate for at least 6 hours in the refrigerator. At the same time, soak the rice for at least 3 hours in cold water.

To make the sauce, pound the coriander root, garlic, chilli and a pinch of salt to a paste using a mortar and pestle. Combine the vinegar, palm sugar and 185 ml (6 fl oz/¾ cup) water in a saucepan and stir until the sugar has dissolved. Bring to the boil, then add the paste and cook for 8–10 minutes, or until reduced by half. Set aside until ready to serve.

Drain the rice well, then line a bamboo steamer with muslin or banana leaves, spread the rice over and cover with a tight-fitting lid. Steam over a wok or large saucepan of boiling water for 40 minutes, or until the rice is translucent, sticky and tender. If steam is escaping, wrap some foil over the top of the steamer. Keep covered until ready to serve.

Meanwhile, heat a barbecue to medium heat, then cook the chicken, turning regularly for about 25 minutes, or until tender and cooked through. The breast pieces may only take about 15 minutes so take them off first and keep warm.

Serve the chicken, rice, dipping sauce and cucumber on separate plates in the centre of the table and allow your guests to help themselves.

Thai Duck and Pineapple Curry

※ SERVES 4–6
※ PREPARATION TIME: 10 MINUTES
※ COOKING TIME: 15 MINUTES

1 tablespoon peanut oil
8 spring onions (scallions), sliced
    diagonally into 3 cm (1¼ inch) lengths
2 garlic cloves, crushed
2–4 tablespoons Thai red curry paste
750 g (1 lb 10 oz) Chinese roast duck,
    chopped
400 ml (14 fl oz) coconut milk
450 g (1 lb) tinned pineapple pieces in
    syrup, drained
3 kaffir lime leaves
3 tablespoons chopped coriander (cilantro)
    leaves
2 tablespoons chopped mint

Heat a wok until very hot, add the oil and swirl to coat. Add the spring onion, garlic and red curry paste, and stir-fry for 1 minute, or until fragrant.

Add the duck pieces, coconut milk, pineapple pieces, kaffir lime leaves, and half the coriander and mint. Bring to the boil, then reduce the heat and simmer for 10 minutes, or until the duck is heated through and the sauce has thickened slightly. Stir in the remaining coriander and mint, and serve with jasmine rice.

Duck Breast with Walnut and Pomegranate Sauce

※ SERVES 4
※ PREPARATION TIME: 15 MINUTES
※ COOKING TIME: 25 MINUTES

4 large duck breasts
1 onion, finely chopped
250 ml (9 fl oz/1 cup) fresh pomegranate
    juice
2 tablespoons lemon juice
2 tablespoons soft brown sugar
1 teaspoon ground cinnamon
185 g (6½ oz/1½ cups) chopped walnuts
pomegranate seeds, to garnish (optional)

Preheat the oven to 180°C (350°F/Gas 4). Score each duck breast two or three times on the skin side. Cook in a non-stick frying pan over high heat, skin side down, for 6 minutes, or until crisp and most of the fat has been rendered. Put in an ovenproof dish. Remove all but 1 tablespoon of fat from the pan. Add the onion to the pan and cook over medium heat for 2–3 minutes, or until golden. Add the pomegranate juice, lemon juice, sugar, cinnamon and 125 g (4½ oz/ 1 cup) of the walnuts and cook for 1 minute. Pour over the duck and bake for 15 minutes. Rest the duck for 5 minutes. Skim any excess fat from the sauce. Slice the duck and serve with the sauce. Garnish with the pomegranate seeds and the remaining walnuts.

Thai Duck and Pineapple Curry

Roast Pheasant

* SERVES 4–6
* PREPARATION TIME: 20 MINUTES
* COOKING TIME: 1 HOUR

2 x 1 kg (2 lb 4 oz) pheasants
6 thin bacon slices
8 sprigs thyme
80 g (2¾ oz) butter, melted
2 apples, cored and cut into thick wedges
60 ml (2 fl oz/¼ cup) apple cider
125 ml (4 fl oz/½ cup) cream
2 teaspoons thyme leaves
2–4 teaspoons apple cider vinegar

Preheat the oven to 230°C (450°C/Gas 8). Rinse the pheasants and pat dry. Tuck the wings underneath the pheasants and tie the legs together with kitchen string. Wrap the bacon around each pheasant and secure with toothpicks. Thread the thyme sprigs through the bacon. Dip 2 large pieces of muslin into the melted butter and wrap one around each pheasant.

Place on a rack in a baking dish and bake for 10 minutes. Reduce the oven to 200°C (400°C/Gas 6) and bake for a further 35 minutes. About 20 minutes before the end of the cooking, add the apple wedges to the base of the dish. The pheasants are cooked when the juices run clear when pierced with a skewer. Remove the pheasants and apple wedges, discard the muslin and toothpicks, then cover and keep warm.

Place the baking dish with the juices on the stovetop. Pour the apple cider into the pan and bring to the boil. Cook for 3 minutes, or until reduced by half. Strain into a clean saucepan. Add the cream to the saucepan and boil for 5 minutes, or until the sauce thickens slightly. Stir in the thyme leaves and season well. Add the apple cider vinegar, to taste. Serve with the pheasant and apple.

Indonesian Spicy Chicken Soup

❧ SERVES 6
❧ PREPARATION TIME: 30 MINUTES
❧ COOKING TIME: 2 HOURS

2 teaspoons coriander seeds
2 tablespoons vegetable oil
1.4 kg (3 lb 2 oz) whole chicken, jointed
    into 8 pieces
4 garlic cloves
1 onion, chopped
2 teaspoons finely sliced ginger
1 dried red chilli, halved
2 lemongrass stems, white part only,
    roughly chopped
50 g (1¾ oz) coriander (cilantro) roots
    and stems, well rinsed, roughly
    chopped
2 teaspoons ground turmeric
1 teaspoon galangal powder
1 teaspoon sugar
1 teaspoon ground coriander
1 litre (35 fl oz/4 cups) chicken stock
2 tablespoons lemon juice
120 g (4¼ oz) cellophane noodles
1½ tablespoons fish sauce
90 g (3¼ oz/1 cup) bean sprouts,
    trimmed
3 tablespoons chopped coriander (cilantro)
    leaves
4 spring onions (scallions), thinly sliced
20 g (¾ oz/¼ cup) crisp-fried onions
1 tablespoon sambal oelek

Dry-fry the coriander seeds in a small frying pan over medium heat for 1 minute, or until fragrant. Cool, then finely grind using a mortar and pestle.

Heat a wok to very hot, add 2 teaspoons of the oil and swirl to coat the base and side. Add the chicken pieces and cook in batches for 3–4 minutes, or until browned all over. Remove from the wok and set aside.

Heat the remaining oil in the wok, then add the garlic, onion, ginger and chilli and stir-fry for 5 minutes, or until softened. Add the lemongrass, coriander root and stem, turmeric, galangal, sugar and ground coriander and cook for 5 minutes. Return the chicken to the wok and pour in the stock, lemon juice and 500 ml (17 fl oz/2 cups) water to cover the chicken. Cover the wok with a lid and simmer for 20 minutes, skimming the surface periodically to remove any scum that rises to the top. Remove only the chicken breast pieces, then cover the wok and simmer (still skimming the surface occasionally) for 20 minutes before removing the rest of the chicken pieces. Cover and refrigerate the chicken until needed. Return the lid to the wok and simmer the broth over low heat for 1 hour. Strain through a fine sieve, and allow to cool to room temperature before covering with plastic wrap and refrigerating overnight.

Soak the cellophane noodles in boiling water for 3–4 minutes, then drain and rinse.

Remove any fat from the top of the cold broth. Remove the flesh from the chicken and shred with a fork. Combine the broth and chicken flesh in the wok, and place over medium heat. Bring to the boil, then stir in the fish sauce, bean sprouts, coriander leaves and noodles. Season well, then ladle into large bowls. Sprinkle with spring onion and crisp-fried onion, and serve with sambal oelek.

Clay Pot Chicken and Vegetables

❀ SERVES 4
❀ PREPARATION TIME: 20 MINUTES
❀ COOKING TIME: 25 MINUTES

500 g (1 lb 2 oz) boneless, skinless
   chicken thighs
1 tablespoon soy sauce
1 tablespoon dry sherry
6 dried Chinese mushrooms
2 tablespoons peanut oil
2 small leeks, white part only, sliced
5 cm (2 inch) piece ginger, grated
125 ml (4 fl oz/½ cup) chicken stock
1 teaspoon sesame oil
250 g (9 oz) orange sweet potato, sliced
3 teaspoons cornflour (cornstarch)
steamed rice, to serve

Wash the chicken under cold water and pat it dry
with paper towel. Cut the chicken into small pieces.
Put it in a dish with the soy sauce and sherry, cover
and marinate for 30 minutes in the refrigerator.

Cover the mushrooms with hot water and soak for
20 minutes. Drain and squeeze to remove any excess
liquid. Remove the stems and chop the caps into shreds.

Drain the chicken, reserving the marinade. Heat half
the oil in a wok, swirling gently to coat the base and
side. Add half the chicken pieces and stir-fry briefly
until seared on all sides. Transfer the chicken to a
flameproof clay pot or casserole dish. Stir-fry the
remaining chicken and add it to the clay pot.

Heat the remaining oil in the wok. Add the leek and
ginger and stir-fry for 1 minute. Add the mushrooms,
remaining marinade, stock and sesame oil and cook for
2 minutes. Transfer to the clay pot with the sweet potato
and cook, covered, on the top of the stove over very low
heat for about 20 minutes.

Dissolve the cornflour in a little water and add it to the
pot. Cook, stirring over high heat, until the mixture
boils and thickens. Serve the chicken and vegetables at
once with steamed rice.

NOTE: Like all stews, this is best cooked 1–2 days ahead and
stored, covered, in the refrigerator to allow the flavours to mature.
It can also be frozen, but omit the sweet potato. Steam or boil the
potato separately when the dish is reheating and stir it through.

Roast Duck with Rice Noodles

❧ SERVES 4–6

❧ PREPARATION TIME: 30 MINUTES

❧ COOKING TIME: 45 MINUTES

15 g (½ oz) dried Chinese mushrooms

40 g (1½ oz) wood ear fungus (see Note)

1 whole Chinese roast duck

1 tablespoon vegetable oil

2 teaspoons sesame oil

1 garlic clove, crushed

1 tablespoon grated fresh ginger

115 g (4 oz) fresh baby corn, cut in half
  diagonally

2 spring onions (scallions), thinly sliced

200 g (7 oz) snow peas (mangetout), cut
  in half diagonally

400 g (14 oz) bok choy (pak choy), cut
  into 2 cm (¾ inch) lengths

100 ml (3½ fl oz) oyster sauce

1 long red chilli, seeded and finely sliced

1.25 litres (44 fl oz/5 cups) chicken stock

1 tablespoon chopped coriander
  (cilantro) leaves

1 tablespoon torn Thai basil leaves

400 g (14 oz) fresh rice noodle sheets, cut
  into 2 cm (¾ inch) strips

Put the Chinese mushrooms in a heatproof bowl, cover with boiling water and soak for 30 minutes. Squeeze the mushrooms dry, discard the stems and finely chop the caps. Put the wood ear fungus in a heatproof bowl, cover with boiling water and soak for 20 minutes, or until soft. Drain and cut into bite-sized pieces.

Remove the meat from the duck and slice thinly. Put the bones in a large saucepan with 2.75 litres (96 fl oz/ 11 cups) water. Bring to the boil over high heat. Reduce the heat and simmer for 30 minutes. Remove any scum from the surface, then strain through a fine sieve.

Heat a wok over high heat, add the vegetable and sesame oils and swirl to coat the base and side. Add the garlic and ginger and fry for 30 seconds. Add the duck meat and stir-fry for 1 minute. Add the Chinese mushrooms, wood ear fungus, corn, spring onion, snow peas and bok choy and stir-fry for 2 minutes. Stir in the oyster sauce, chilli and stock and simmer for 2 minutes, or until heated through. Stir in the herbs.

Cover the noodles with boiling water and soak for 1–2 minutes, or until tender. Separate gently and drain. Divide among the bowls, then ladle the soup on top.

Note: Wood ear (also called black fungus) is a cultivated wood fungus. It is mainly available dried; it needs to be reconstituted in boiling water for a few minutes until it expands to five times its dried size, before cooking.

Japanese Udon Miso Soup with Chicken

❧ SERVES 4–6

❧ PREPARATION TIME: 35 MINUTES

❧ COOKING TIME: 10 MINUTES

8 dried shiitake mushrooms

250 ml (9 fl oz/1 cup) boiling water

400 g (14 oz) fresh udon noodles

1 litre (35 fl oz/4 cups) chicken stock

600 g (1 lb 5 oz) boneless, skinless
   chicken breast, cut into 1.5 cm
   (⅝ inch) thick strips

300 g (10½ oz) baby bok choy (pak choy),
   halved lengthways

60 g (2¼ oz/¼ cup) white miso paste

2 teaspoons dashi granules

1 tablespoon wakame flakes or other
   seaweed

150 g (5½ oz) silken firm tofu, cut into
   1 cm (½ inch) cubes

3 spring onions (scallions), sliced
   diagonally

Soak the mushrooms in the boiling water for 20 minutes. Squeeze dry, reserving the soaking liquid. Discard the woody stalks and thinly slice the caps. Set aside.

Bring 2 litres (70 fl oz/8 cups) water to the boil in a large saucepan and cook the noodles for 1–2 minutes, or until tender. Drain immediately and rinse under cold water. Set aside.

Pour the stock and 1 litre (35 fl oz/4 cups) water into a wok and bring to the boil, then reduce the heat and simmer. Add the chicken and cook for 2–3 minutes, or until almost cooked through.

Add the mushrooms and cook for 1 minute. Add the bok choy halves and simmer for a further minute, or until beginning to wilt, then add the miso paste, dashi granules, wakame and reserved mushroom liquid. Stir to dissolve the dashi and miso paste. Do not allow to boil.

Gently stir in the tofu. Distribute the noodles among the serving bowls then ladle the hot soup over them. Sprinkle with the spring onion.

Kung Pao Chicken

❀ SERVES 4
❀ PREPARATION TIME: 15 MINUTES
❀ COOKING TIME: 10 MINUTES

1 egg white
2 teaspoons cornflour (cornstarch)
$^1/_2$ teaspoon sesame oil
2 teaspoons Chinese rice wine
1 $^1/_2$ tablespoons soy sauce
600 g (1 lb 5 oz) boneless, skinless
   chicken thighs, cut into small cubes
60 ml (2 fl oz/$^1/_4$ cup) chicken stock
2 teaspoons Chinese black vinegar
1 teaspoon soft brown sugar
2 tablespoons vegetable oil
3 long dried red chillies, cut in half
   lengthways
3 garlic cloves, finely chopped
2 teaspoons finely grated fresh ginger
2 spring onions (scallions), thinly sliced
50 g (1$^3/_4$ oz/$^1/_3$ cup) unsalted raw
   peanuts, roughly crushed

Lightly whisk together the egg white, cornflour, sesame oil, rice wine and 2 teaspoons of the soy sauce in a large non-metallic bowl. Add the chicken and toss to coat in the marinade. Cover with plastic wrap and marinate in the refrigerator for 30 minutes.

To make the stir-fry sauce, combine the stock, vinegar, sugar and the remaining soy sauce in a small bowl.

Heat a wok over high heat, add 1 tablespoon of the vegetable oil and swirl to coat the base and side. Stir-fry the chicken in batches for about 3 minutes, or until browned. Remove from the wok.

Heat the remaining oil in the wok, then add the chilli and cook for 15 seconds, or until it starts to change colour. Add the garlic, ginger, spring onion and peanuts and stir-fry for 1 minute. Return the chicken to the wok along with the stir-fry sauce and stir-fry for 3 minutes, or until heated through and the sauce has thickened slightly. Serve immediately.

NOTE: This dish is said to have been created for an important court official called Kung Pao (or Gong Bao), who was stationed in the Sichuan province of China. It is characterised by the flavours of the long, dried red chillies, popular in Sichuan cuisine, and the crunchy texture of the peanuts. This dish can also be made with meat or prawns (shrimp).

Braised Duck with Mushrooms

❋ SERVES 6
❋ PREPARATION TIME: 20 MINUTES
❋ COOKING TIME: 1 HOUR 10 MINUTES

15 g (½ oz) dried Chinese mushrooms
1.5 kg (3 lb 5 oz) whole duck
2 teaspoons vegetable oil
2 tablespoons soy sauce
2 tablespoons Chinese rice wine
2 teaspoons sugar
2 wide strips orange peel
125 g (4½ oz) watercress

Soak the mushrooms in hot water for 20 minutes. Drain well, discard the stems and thinly slice the caps.

Using a large heavy knife or cleaver, chop the duck into small pieces, cutting through the bone. Arrange the pieces on a rack and pour boiling water over them — the water will plump up the skin and help keep the duck succulent. Drain and pat dry with paper towel.

Heat the oil in a wok over medium heat and add the duck. Cook, in batches, for about 8 minutes, turning regularly, until browned. (The darker the browning at this stage, the better the colour when finished.) Between each batch, wipe out the pan with crumpled paper towel to remove excess oil.

Wipe the pan with paper towel again and return all the duck to the pan. Add the mushrooms, soy sauce, wine, sugar and orange peel. Bring the mixture to the boil, reduce the heat, cover and simmer gently for 35 minutes or until the duck is tender. Season to taste and stand for 10 minutes, covered, before serving.

Remove the duck from the sauce and discard the orange peel. Pick off small sprigs of the watercress and arrange them on one side of a large serving platter. Carefully place the duck segments on the other side of the plate — try not to place the duck on the watercress as it will become soggy. Carefully spoon a little of the sauce over the duck and serve.

NOTE: Braising the duck over low heat produces tender, melt-in-the-mouth meat and a delicious sauce. If the heat is too high, the duck will dry out and lose its flavour.

Roast Goose

❀ SERVES 6
❀ PREPARATION TIME: 15 MINUTES
❀ COOKING TIME: 1 HOUR 30 MINUTES

3 kg (6 lb 12 oz) goose

GRAVY
1 tablespoon plain (all-purpose) flour
2 tablespoons brandy
375 ml (13 fl oz/1 1/2 cups) chicken stock

BREAD SAUCE
1 small onion, sliced
310 ml (10 3/4 fl oz/1 1/4 cups) milk
1 bay leaf
4 black peppercorns
2 whole cloves
100 g (3 1/2 oz/1 1/4 cups) fresh breadcrumbs
pinch freshly grated nutmeg
20 g (3/4 oz) butter

Preheat the oven to 180°C (350°F/Gas 4). Remove any excess fat from inside the cavity of the goose. Put the goose in a large pan, cover with boiling water, then drain. Dry with paper towels. Put the goose, breast side down, on a rack in a very large baking dish. Using a fine skewer, prick the skin of the goose all over. Bake for 1 hour, then remove from the oven and drain off any excess fat. Turn the goose over and bake for a further 30 minutes, or until golden. Remove from the baking dish, cover with foil and leave for 5–10 minutes.

To make the gravy, drain all except 2 tablespoons of fat from the baking dish and put the dish on the stovetop over low heat. Add the flour and stir over medium heat until well browned. Gradually stir in the brandy and chicken stock. Stir until the gravy boils and thickens. Season.

To make the sauce, combine the onion, milk, bay leaf, peppercorns and cloves in a saucepan. Bring to the boil over medium heat, then reduce the heat and simmer for 10 minutes. Strain into a bowl and discard the onion and flavourings. Add the breadcrumbs, nutmeg and butter. Stir, then season.

Chicken Gumbo

- SERVES 4–6
- PREPARATION TIME: 15 MINUTES
- COOKING TIME: 2 HOURS 30 MINUTES

80 ml (2½ fl oz/⅓ cup) vegetable oil

30 g (1 oz/¼ cup) plain (all-purpose)
   flour

600 g (1 lb 5 oz) boneless, skinless
   chicken thighs

60 g (2¼ oz) unsalted butter

100 g (3½ oz) smoked ham, diced

150 g (5½ oz) chorizo, thinly sliced

2 onions, chopped

2 garlic cloves, finely chopped

2 celery stalks, thinly sliced

1 red capsicum (pepper), seeded,
   membrane removed and finely chopped

450 g (1 lb) tomatoes, peeled, seeded and
   roughly chopped

500 ml (17 fl oz/2 cups) chicken stock

1 bay leaf

2 teaspoons thyme

Tabasco sauce, to taste

350 g (12 oz) okra, cut into 1 cm
   (½ inch) slices

2 spring onions (scallions), sliced
   (optional)

2 tablespoons chopped flat-leaf (Italian)
   parsley (optional)

Heat 3 tablespoons of the oil in a small, heavy-based saucepan, add the flour and stir to make a smooth paste. Stir over very low heat for 1 hour, or until the roux turns very dark brown, but is not burnt. This requires a great deal of patience and stirring but provides the gumbo with its dark look and rich flavour — when it is done, the roux should be the colour of dark chocolate. Remove from the heat.

Pat the chicken thighs dry with paper towels, cut into quarters and lightly season. Heat the remaining oil and half the butter in a heavy-based frying pan over medium heat. Cook the chicken for about 5 minutes, or until golden brown. Remove the chicken with a slotted spoon. Add the ham and chorizo and cook for 4–5 minutes, or until lightly golden. Remove, leaving as much rendered fat in the pan as possible.

Add the remaining butter to the same pan and cook the onion, garlic, celery and capsicum over medium heat for 5–6 minutes, or until the vegetables have softened but not browned. Transfer the vegetables to a heavy-based, flameproof casserole dish. Add the tomato and the roux and stir well. Gradually stir the stock into the pan. Add the herbs and season with the Tabasco. Bring to the boil, stirring constantly. Reduce the heat, add the chicken, ham and chorizo to the casserole dish and simmer, uncovered, for 1 hour. Add the okra and cook for a further hour. Skim the surface as the gumbo cooks because the chorizo will produce a lot of oil. The gumbo should thicken considerably in the last 20 minutes as the okra softens. Remove the bay leaf and serve. Garnish with spring onion and parsley, if desired.

NOTE: Gumbo is a speciality of Cajun cuisine and is a cross between a soup and a stew. Traditionally, gumbo is served in deep bowls, each containing a few tablespoons of cooked rice in the bottom.

Chicken and Chorizo Paella

※ SERVES 6
※ PREPARATION TIME: 30 MINUTES
※ COOKING TIME: 1 HOUR 5 MINUTES

60 ml (2 fl oz/¼ cup) olive oil
1 large red capsicum (pepper), cut into
    5 mm (¼ inch) strips
600 g (1 lb 5 oz) boneless, skinless
    chicken thighs, cut into 3 cm (1¼ inch)
    cubes
200 g (7 oz) chorizo, cut into 2 cm
    (¾ inch) slices
200 g (7 oz) mushrooms, thinly sliced
3 garlic cloves, crushed
1 tablespoon grated lemon zest
700 g (1 lb 9 oz) ripe tomatoes, roughly
    chopped
200 g (7 oz) green beans, trimmed and cut
    into 3 cm (1¼ inch) lengths
1 tablespoon chopped rosemary
2 tablespoons chopped flat-leaf (Italian)
    parsley
¼ teaspoon saffron threads dissolved in
    60 ml (2 fl oz/¼ cup) hot water
440 g (15½ oz/2 cups) short-grain white
    rice
750 ml (26 fl oz/3 cups) hot chicken stock
6 lemon wedges, to serve

Heat the oil in a paella pan or in a large, heavy-based, deep frying pan over medium heat. Add the capsicum strips and cook, stirring, for about 6 minutes, or until softened, then remove from the pan.

Add the chicken to the pan and cook for 10 minutes, or until browned. Remove from the pan. Add the chorizo to the pan and cook for 5 minutes, or until golden. Remove from the pan. Add the mushrooms, garlic and lemon zest to the pan, and cook over medium heat for 5 minutes.

Stir in the tomato and capsicum, and cook for a further 5 minutes, or until the tomato is soft.

Add the beans, rosemary, parsley, saffron mixture, rice, chicken and chorizo. Stir briefly and add the stock. Do not stir at this point. Reduce the heat and simmer for 30 minutes. Remove from the heat, cover and leave to stand for 10 minutes. Serve with lemon wedges.

NOTE: Paella pans are available from specialist kitchenware shops.

Butter Chicken

☙ SERVES 4–6
☙ PREPARATION TIME: 10 MINUTES
☙ COOKING TIME: 35 MINUTES

2 tablespoons peanut oil
1 kg (2 lb 4 oz) boneless, skinless chicken
   thighs, quartered
60 g (2¼ oz) clarified butter or ghee
2 teaspoons garam masala
2 teaspoons sweet paprika
2 teaspoons ground coriander
1 tablespoon finely chopped fresh ginger
¼ teaspoon chilli powder
1 cinnamon stick
6 cardamom pods, bruised
350 g (12 oz) tomato passata (puréed
   tomatoes)
1 tablespoon sugar
60 g (2¼ oz/¼ cup) plain yoghurt
125 ml (4 fl oz/½ cup) cream
1 tablespoon lemon juice
poppadoms, to serve

Heat a wok to very hot, add 1 tablespoon of the oil and swirl to coat the base and side. Add half the chicken and stir-fry for about 4 minutes, or until nicely browned. Remove from the wok. Add a little extra oil, if needed, and brown the remaining chicken. Remove from the wok and set aside.

Reduce the heat to medium, add the butter and stir until melted. Add the garam masala, paprika, coriander, ginger, chilli powder, cinnamon stick and cardamom pods, and stir-fry for 1 minute, or until the spices are fragrant. Return the chicken to the wok and mix in until coated in the spices. Add the tomato and sugar and simmer, stirring, for 15 minutes, or until the chicken is tender and the sauce is thick. Stir in the yoghurt, cream and lemon juice and simmer for 5 minutes, or until the sauce has thickened slightly. Serve with poppadoms.

Chicken Mulligatawny

❧ SERVES 6
❧ PREPARATION TIME: 25 MINUTES
❧ COOKING TIME: 4 HOURS

STOCK

1.5 kg (3 lb 5 oz) chicken
1 carrot, chopped
2 celery stalks, chopped
4 spring onions (scallions), chopped
2 cm (¾ inch) piece of fresh ginger, sliced

20 g (¾ oz) clarified butter or ghee
1 large onion, finely chopped
3 garlic cloves, crushed
8 curry leaves
55 g (2 oz/¼ cup) Madras curry paste
250 g (9 oz/1 cup) red lentils, washed
   and drained
2 tomatoes, peeled, seeded and roughly
   chopped
75 g (2¾ oz/⅓ cup) short-grain rice
250 ml (9 fl oz/1 cup) coconut cream
2 tablespoons coriander (cilantro) leaves,
   chopped
mango chutney, to serve

To make the stock, put all the ingredients and 4 litres (140 fl oz/16 cups) cold water in a large stockpot or saucepan. Bring to the boil, removing any scum that rises to the surface. Reduce the heat to low and simmer, partly covered, for 3 hours. Continue to remove any scum from the surface. Carefully remove the chicken and cool. Strain the stock into a bowl and cool. Cover and refrigerate overnight. Discard the skin and bones from the chicken and shred the flesh into small pieces. Cover and refrigerate overnight.

Melt the ghee in a large saucepan over medium heat. Cook the onion for 5 minutes, or until softened but not browned. Add the garlic and curry leaves and cook for 1 minute. Add the curry paste, cook for 1 minute, then stir in the lentils. Pour in the stock and bring to the boil over high heat, removing any scum from the surface. Reduce the heat, add the tomato and simmer for 30 minutes, or until the lentils are soft.

Meanwhile, bring a large saucepan of water to the boil. Add the rice and cook for 12 minutes, stirring once or twice. Drain. Stir the rice into the soup with the chicken and coconut cream until warmed through – don't allow it to boil or it will curdle. Season. Sprinkle with the coriander and serve with the mango chutney.

Roast Chicken Stuffed with Pine Nuts and Rice

❧ SERVES 4–6

❧ PREPARATION TIME: 30 MINUTES

❧ COOKING TIME: 2 HOURS 30 MINUTES

STUFFING

60 g (2¼ oz) clarified butter or ghee,
  melted

1 onion, chopped

1 teaspoon ground allspice

65 g (2½ oz/⅓ cup) basmati rice

30 g (1 oz/¼ cup) walnuts, chopped

50 g (1¾ oz/⅓ cup) pine nuts

40 g (2½ oz/⅓ cup) sultanas (golden
  raisins)

125 ml (4 fl oz/½ cup) chicken stock

1.6 kg (3 lb 8 oz) chicken

170 ml (5½ fl oz/⅔ cup) chicken stock

Preheat the oven to 180°C (350°F/Gas 4). Pour half the butter into a large frying pan, then add the onion and cook for 5 minutes over medium heat until the onion is transparent. Stir in the allspice.

Add the rice and nuts to the pan, then cook for 3–4 minutes over medium–high heat. Add the sultanas, stock and 60 ml (2 fl oz/¼ cup) of water. Bring to boil, then reduce the heat and simmer for 8–10 minutes, until the water is absorbed. Allow to cool.

Rinse the cavity of the chicken with cold water and pat dry inside and out with paper towels.

When the stuffing is cool, spoon it into the cavity. Truss the chicken, using string, then place in a deep baking dish, and rub ½ teaspoon salt and ¼ teaspoon freshly ground black pepper into the skin, using your fingertips.

Pour the remainder of the butter over the chicken, then add the stock to the pan. Roast for 2 hours 10 minutes, basting every 20–25 minutes with juices from the pan. Rest the chicken for 15 minutes before carving. Serve with the stuffing.

Nonya Lime Chicken

❊ SERVES 4–6

❊ PREPARATION TIME: 20 MINUTES

❊ COOKING TIME: 25 MINUTES

CURRY PASTE
75 g (2¾ oz/⅔ cup) red Asian shallots or
    French shallots
4 garlic cloves
2 lemongrass stems, white part only,
    chopped
2 teaspoons finely chopped fresh galangal
1 teaspoon ground turmeric
2 tablespoons sambal oelek
1 tablespoon shrimp paste

60 ml (2 fl oz/¼ cup) vegetable oil
1 kg (2 lb 4 oz) boneless, skinless chicken
    thighs, cut into 3 cm (1¼ inch) cubes
400 ml (14 fl oz) coconut milk
1 teaspoon finely grated lime zest
125 ml (4 fl oz/½ cup) lime juice
6 kaffir lime leaves, finely shredded, plus
    extra, to garnish
2 tablespoons tamarind purée
steamed rice, to serve
lime wedges, to garnish

Combine the curry paste ingredients in a food processor or blender and blend until a smooth paste forms.

Heat a non-stick wok until very hot, add the oil and swirl to coat the base and side. Add the curry paste and stir-fry for 1–2 minutes, or until fragrant. Add the chicken and stir-fry for 5 minutes, or until browned. Add the coconut milk, lime zest and juice, kaffir lime leaves and tamarind purée. Reduce the heat and simmer for 15 minutes, or until the chicken is cooked and the sauce has reduced and thickened slightly. Season well with salt. Serve with steamed rice and garnish with lime wedges and the extra kaffir lime leaves.

meat

Peppered Beef Fillet with Béarnaise Sauce

❧ SERVES 6
❧ PREPARATION TIME: 30 MINUTES
❧ COOKING TIME: 45 MINUTES

1 kg (2 lb 4 oz) beef eye fillet
1 tablespoon oil
2 garlic cloves, crushed
1 tablespoon cracked black peppercorns
2 teaspoons crushed coriander seeds

BÉARNAISE SAUCE
3 spring onions (scallions), chopped
125 ml (4 fl oz/½ cup) dry white wine
2 tablespoons tarragon vinegar
1 tablespoon chopped tarragon
125 g (4½ oz) butter
4 egg yolks
1 tablespoon lemon juice

Preheat the oven to 210°C (415°F/Gas 6–7). Trim the fillet, removing any excess fat. Tie at regular intervals with kitchen string. Combine the oil and garlic, brush over the fillet, then roll the fillet in the combined peppercorns and coriander seeds.

Put the meat on a rack in a baking dish. Bake for 10 minutes, then reduce the oven to 180°C (350°F/Gas 4) and cook for a further 15–20 minutes for a rare result, or until cooked according to taste. Cover and leave for 10–15 minutes. Slice and serve with béarnaise sauce.

To make the béarnaise sauce, put the spring onion, wine, vinegar and tarragon in a saucepan. Boil the mixture until only 2 tablespoons of the liquid remains. Strain and set aside. Melt the butter in a small saucepan. Place the wine mixture in a food processor with the egg yolks, and process for 30 seconds. With the motor running, add the butter in a thin stream, leaving the milky white sediment behind in the saucepan. Process until thickened. Add the lemon juice, to taste, and season.

Lamb Tagine with Quince

❧ SERVES 4–6
❧ PREPARATION TIME: 20 MINUTES
❧ COOKING TIME: 1 HOUR 40 MINUTES

1.5 kg (3 lb 5 oz) lamb shoulder, cut into
    3 cm (1¼ inch) pieces
2 large onions, diced
½ teaspoon ground ginger
½ teaspoon cayenne pepper
¼ teaspoon crushed saffron threads
1 teaspoon ground coriander
1 cinnamon stick
25 g (1 oz) roughly chopped coriander
    (cilantro) leaves
40 g (1½ oz) butter
500 g (1 lb 2 oz) quinces, peeled, cored
    and quartered
100 g (3½ oz) dried apricots
coriander (cilantro) sprigs, extra,
    to garnish

Place the lamb in a heavy-based, flameproof casserole dish and add half the onion, the ginger, cayenne pepper, saffron, ground coriander, cinnamon stick, coriander leaves and some salt and pepper. Cover with cold water and bring to the boil over medium heat. Reduce the heat and simmer, partly covered, for 1½ hours, or until the lamb is tender.

While the lamb is cooking, melt the butter in a heavy-based frying pan and cook the remaining onion and the quince for 15 minutes over medium heat, or until lightly golden.

When the lamb has been cooking for 1 hour, add the quince mixture and apricots and continue cooking.

Taste the sauce and adjust the seasoning if necessary. Transfer to a warm serving dish and sprinkle with coriander sprigs. Serve with couscous or rice.

Pork Sausages with White Beans

❀ SERVES 4
❀ PREPARATION TIME: 25 MINUTES
❀ COOKING TIME: 1 HOUR 40 MINUTES

350 g (12 oz/1¾ cups) dried white
   haricot beans
150 g (5½ oz) tocino, speck or pancetta,
   unsliced
½ leek, white part only, thinly sliced
2 garlic cloves
1 bay leaf
1 small red chilli, split and seeded
1 small onion
2 whole cloves
1 rosemary sprig
3 thyme sprigs
1 flat-leaf (Italian) parsley sprig
60 ml (2 fl oz/¼ cup) olive oil
8 pork sausages
½ onion, finely chopped
1 green capsicum (pepper), seeded and
   membrane removed, finely chopped
½ teaspoon paprika
125 ml (4 fl oz/½ cup) tomato passata
   (puréed tomatoes)
1 teaspoon cider vinegar

Soak the beans overnight in cold water. Drain and rinse the beans under cold water. Put them in a large saucepan with the tocino, leek, garlic, bay leaf and chilli. Stud the onion with the cloves and add to the pan. Tie the rosemary, thyme and parsley together and add to the pan. Pour in 750 ml (26 fl oz/3 cups) cold water and bring to the boil. Add 1 tablespoon of the oil, reduce the heat and simmer, covered, for 1 hour, or until the beans are tender. When necessary, add boiling water to keep the beans covered.

Prick each sausage five or six times and twist tightly in opposite directions in the middle to give two short fat sausages. Put in a single layer in a large frying pan and add enough cold water to reach halfway up their sides. Bring to the boil and simmer, turning a few times, until all the water has evaporated and the sausages brown lightly in the fat that is left in the pan. Remove from the pan and cut the short sausages apart. Add the remaining oil, the chopped onion and capsicum to the pan and fry over medium heat for 5–6 minutes. Stir in the paprika, cook for 30 seconds, then add the passata and season. Cook, stirring, for 1 minute.

Remove the tocino, herb sprigs and any loose large pieces of onion from the bean mixture. Leave in any loose leaves from the herbs, and any small pieces of onion. Add the sausages and sauce to the pan and stir the vinegar through. Bring to the boil. Adjust the seasoning.

Red Cooked Pork Belly

☸ SERVES 6
☸ PREPARATION TIME: 10 MINUTES
☸ COOKING TIME: 2 HOURS 10 MINUTES

6 dried shiitake mushrooms
2 teaspoons peanut oil
1 kg (2 lb 4 oz) piece pork belly
500 ml (17 fl oz/2 cups) chicken stock
60 ml (2 fl oz/¼ cup) dark soy sauce
60 ml (2 fl oz/¼ cup) Chinese rice wine
4 garlic cloves, bruised
5 x 5 cm (2 x 2 inch) piece fresh ginger,
    sliced
1 piece dried mandarin or tangerine peel
2 teaspoons sichuan peppercorns
2 star anise
1 cinnamon stick
1½ tablespoons Chinese rock sugar
    (see Note)
Thai basil sprigs, to garnish

Cover the mushrooms in 250 ml (9 fl oz/1 cup) boiling water and soak for 20 minutes, or until soft. Squeeze dry, reserving the liquid.

Heat a large wok over high heat, add the oil and swirl to coat. Add the pork, skin side down, and cook for 5 minutes, or until well browned, then turn over and cook for a further 6 minutes, or until sealed.

Add the stock, soy sauce, rice wine, garlic, ginger, citrus peel, spices, reserved mushroom soaking liquid and 500 ml (17 fl oz/2 cups) water. Bring to the boil, then reduce the heat to low and simmer, covered, for 1¼ hours.

Add the sugar and mushrooms and cook for a further 45 minutes, or until the pork is very tender. Remove the pork from the stock and cut into slices about 1 cm (½ inch) thick. Strain the liquid into a bowl, then return the strained liquid to the wok. Bring to the boil and continue boiling until reduced to about 185 ml (6 fl oz/¾ cup).

Place the pork on a platter with the mushrooms and spoon on some of the cooking liquid. Garnish with the Thai basil. Serve with steamed rice.

NOTE: Chinese rock sugar is the crystallised form of saturated sugar liquor. It is named for its irregular rock-shaped pieces and imparts a rich flavour, especially to braised or 'red cooked' foods as well as sweets, glazing them with a translucent sheen. Available in the Asian section of large supermarkets, or in Asian grocery stores.

Surf 'n' Turf

❄ SERVES 4
❄ PREPARATION TIME: 20 MINUTES
❄ COOKING TIME: 15–20 MINUTES

LEMON MUSTARD SAUCE
30 g (1 oz) butter
1 spring onion (scallion), finely chopped
1 garlic clove, crushed
1 tablespoon plain (all-purpose) flour
250 ml (9 fl oz/1 cup) milk
2 tablespoons cream
1 tablespoon lemon juice
2 teaspoons dijon mustard

1 large or 2 small raw lobster tails
2 tablespoons olive oil
4 beef eye fillets (200 g/7 oz each)
175 g (6 oz) fresh or frozen crabmeat
flat-leaf (Italian) parsley, to garnish

To make the sauce, melt the butter in a saucepan, add the spring onion and garlic and stir over medium heat for 1 minute, or until the onion has softened. Stir in the flour and cook for 1 minute, or until pale and foaming. Remove from the heat and gradually stir in the milk. Return to the heat and stir constantly until the sauce boils and thickens. Reduce the heat and simmer for 2 minutes. Remove from the heat and stir in the cream, lemon juice and mustard. Keep warm.

Starting at the end where the head was, cut down each side of the lobster shell on the underside with kitchen scissors. Pull back the flap and remove the meat from the shell. Heat half the oil in a frying pan, add the lobster meat and cook over medium heat for 3 minutes each side (longer if using a large tail), or until just cooked through. Remove from the pan and keep warm. Reserve the oil in the pan.

Meanwhile, heat the remaining oil in a separate frying pan, add the steaks and cook over high heat for 2 minutes each side to seal, turning once. For rare steaks, cook each side 1 more minute. For medium and well-done steaks, reduce the heat to medium and continue cooking for 2–3 minutes each side for medium or 4–6 minutes each side for well done. Remove from the pan and keep warm.

Add the crabmeat to the reserved oil in the lobster pan and stir until heated through. To serve, place the steaks on plates. Top with crab followed by slices of lobster. Pour the sauce over the top and garnish with parsley.

Lamb Korma

❀ SERVES 4–6
❀ PREPARATION TIME: 30 MINUTES
❀ COOKING TIME: 1 HOUR

2 kg (4 lb 8 oz) leg of lamb, boned
1 onion, chopped
2 teaspoons grated fresh ginger
3 garlic cloves
1 tablespoon coriander seeds
2 teaspoons ground cumin
1 teaspoon cardamom pods
large pinch cayenne pepper
2 tablespoons ghee or vegetable oil
1 onion, extra, thinly sliced
2 tablespoons tomato paste (concentrated
    purée)
125 g (4½ oz/½ cup) plain yoghurt
spring onions (scallions), sliced, to garnish
steamed rice, to serve

Remove all excess fat, skin and sinew from the lamb. Cut the meat into 3 cm (1¼ inch) cubes and put in a large bowl.

Put the chopped onion, the ginger, garlic, coriander seeds, cumin, cardamom pods, cayenne pepper and ½ teaspoon salt in a food processor and process until the mixture forms a smooth paste. Add the spice mixture to the lamb. Mix well to coat. Set aside for 1 hour.

Heat the ghee or oil in a large frying pan. Add the sliced onion and cook, stirring, over medium–low heat until the onion is soft. Add the lamb mixture and cook for 8–10 minutes, stirring constantly, until the lamb is browned all over. Add tomato paste and 2 tablespoons of the yoghurt, and stir until combined. Simmer, uncovered, until the liquid has been absorbed. Add the remaining yoghurt, 2 tablespoons at a time, stirring until the mixture is nearly dry between each addition. Cover the pan and simmer over low heat for 30 minutes, or until the meat is tender, stirring occasionally. Add a little water if the mixture becomes too dry. Garnish with spring onion and serve with steamed rice.

Rabbit with Rosemary and White Wine

❧ SERVES 4
❧ PREPARATION TIME: 25 MINUTES
❧ COOKING TIME: 2 HOURS

1 large rabbit (about 1.6 kg/3 lb 8 oz)
30 g (1 oz/¼ cup) seasoned flour
60 ml (2 fl oz/¼ cup) olive oil
2 onions, thinly sliced
1 large rosemary sprig
1 small sage sprig
2 garlic cloves, crushed
500 ml (17 fl oz/2 cups) dry white wine
400 g (14 oz) tinned chopped tomatoes
pinch cayenne pepper
125 ml (4 fl oz/½ cup) chicken stock
12 small black olives, such as niçoise or
    Ligurian (optional)
3 small rosemary sprigs, extra (optional)

Cut the rabbit into large pieces and dredge the pieces in the flour. Heat the oil in a large heavy-based saucepan over medium heat. Brown the rabbit pieces on all sides, then remove from the pan.

Reduce the heat and add the onion, rosemary and sage to the saucepan. Cook gently for 10 minutes, then stir in the garlic and return the rabbit to the pan.

Increase the heat to high, add the wine to the pan and cook for 1 minute. Stir in the tomato, the cayenne pepper and half the stock. Reduce the heat, cover and simmer over low heat for 1½ hours, or until the rabbit is tender. Halfway through cooking, check the sauce and if it seems too dry, add the remaining stock. Discard the herb sprigs. Season to taste. Garnish with the olives and extra rosemary, if desired.

Chinese Lamb, Garlic Chive and Cellophane Noodle Soup

❀ SERVES 4
❀ PREPARATION TIME: 10 MINUTES
❀ COOKING TIME: 20 MINUTES

2 tablespoons light soy sauce
1 tablespoon oyster sauce
1 tablespoon Chinese rice wine
1 teaspoon sugar
1¼ teaspoons sesame oil
3 slices fresh ginger plus 1 tablespoon
    finely chopped ginger
250 g (9 oz) lamb fillet
100 g (3½ oz) cellophane noodles
1 tablespoon vegetable oil
2 spring onions (scallions), finely chopped,
    plus extra, to serve
125 g (4½ oz) snipped garlic chives
1 litre (35 fl oz/4 cups) chicken stock

Combine the soy sauce, oyster sauce, rice wine, sugar, ¼ teaspoon of the sesame oil and the ginger slices in a bowl. Add the lamb and marinate for 3 hours, turning occasionally. Remove the lamb and ginger from the marinade with tongs. Set aside.

Meanwhile, soak the noodles in a bowl of boiling water for 3–4 minutes. Rinse, drain and set aside.

Heat a wok over high heat, add the vegetable oil and the remaining sesame oil and swirl to coat the base and side. Add the chopped ginger, spring onion and garlic chives and cook for 30 seconds, stirring constantly. Slowly pour in the stock then bring to the boil. Add the lamb and ginger slices, reduce the heat to low, cover with a lid and poach the lamb for 10 minutes.

Remove the lamb from the wok. Bring the soup to the boil over medium heat. Meanwhile, thinly slice the lamb. Return the sliced lamb to the wok and add the noodles at the same time, stirring well until mixed together. Serve hot with the extra spring onion scattered over the top.

Pork with Apple and Prune Stuffing

❀ SERVES 8

❀ PREPARATION TIME: 35 MINUTES

❀ COOKING TIME: 2 HOURS 10 MINUTES

1 green apple, chopped
75 g (3¼ oz/⅓ cup) pitted and chopped
    prunes
2 tablespoons port
1 tablespoon chopped flat-leaf (Italian)
    parsley
2 kg (4 lb 8 oz) piece boned pork loin
olive oil and salt, to rub on pork

GRAVY WITH WINE
2 tablespoons plain (all-purpose) flour
2 teaspoons worcestershire sauce
2 tablespoons red or white wine
560 ml (19¼ fl oz/2¼ cups) beef or
    chicken stock

Preheat the oven to 240°C (475°F/Gas 8). To make the stuffing, combine the apple, prunes, port and parsley. Lay the pork loin on a board with the rind underneath. Spread the stuffing over the meat side of the loin, roll up and secure with skewers or string at regular intervals. If some of the filling falls out while tying, carefully push it back in. Score the pork rind with a sharp knife at 1 cm (½ inch) intervals (if the butcher hasn't already done so) and rub generously with oil and salt.

Place on a rack in a baking dish. Bake for 15 minutes, then reduce the heat to 180°C (350°F/Gas 4) and bake for 1½–2 hours, or until the pork is cooked through. The juices will run clear when a skewer is inserted into the thickest part of the meat. Cover and stand for 15 minutes before removing the skewers or string and carving. Reserve any pan juices for making the gravy.

To make the gravy, discard all but 2 tablespoons of the pan juices from the baking dish the roast was cooked in. Heat the dish on the stovetop over medium heat, stir in the flour and cook, stirring, until well browned. Remove from the heat and gradually add the worcestershire sauce, wine and stock. Return to the heat. Stir until the mixture boils and thickens, then simmer for 2 minutes. Season with salt and pepper, to taste.

NOTE: If the rind does not crackle, carefully remove it from the meat, cutting between the fat layer and the meat. Scrape off any excess fat and place the rind on a piece of foil. Place it under a hot grill (broiler), and grill until the rind has crackled. Alternatively, place the rind between several sheets of paper towel and microwave on high in 1 minute bursts, for 2–3 minutes in total. The timing will depend on the thickness of the rind.

Chinese Beef and Black Bean Sauce

* SERVES 4–6
* PREPARATION TIME: 15 MINUTES
* COOKING TIME: 20 MINUTES

2 tablespoons rinsed and drained black
    beans, chopped
1 tablespoon dark soy sauce
1 tablespoon Chinese rice wine
1 garlic clove, finely chopped
1 teaspoon sugar
60 ml (2 fl oz/¼ cup) peanut oil
1 onion, cut into wedges
500 g (1 lb 2 oz) lean beef fillet, thinly
    sliced across the grain
½ teaspoon finely chopped fresh ginger
1 teaspoon cornflour (cornstarch)
1 teaspoon sesame oil
steamed rice, to serve

Put the beans, soy sauce, rice wine and 60 ml
(2 fl oz/¼ cup) water in a small bowl and mix.
In a separate bowl, crush the garlic and sugar to a
paste, using a mortar and pestle.

Heat a wok over high heat, add 1 teaspoon of the
peanut oil and swirl to coat the base and side. Add the
onion and stir-fry for 1–2 minutes, then transfer to a
bowl and set aside. Add 1 tablespoon of the peanut oil
to the wok and swirl to coat the base and side, then add
half the beef and stir-fry for 5–6 minutes, or until
browned. Remove to the bowl with the onion. Repeat
with the remaining beef.

Add the remaining peanut oil to the wok along with the
garlic paste and ginger and stir-fry for 30 seconds, or
until fragrant. Add the bean mixture, and the onion
and beef. Bring to the boil, then reduce the heat and
simmer, covered, for 2 minutes.

Combine the cornflour with 1 tablespoon water, pour
into the wok and stir until the sauce boils and thickens.
Stir in the sesame oil and serve with steamed rice.

Veal Cooked with Vinegar

⚜ SERVES 6–8
⚜ PREPARATION TIME: 10 MINUTES
⚜ COOKING TIME: 1 HOUR 50 MINUTES

60 g (2¼ oz/½ cup) plain (all-purpose)
    flour
large pinch cayenne pepper
1 kg (2 lb 4 oz) veal steaks
60 ml (2 fl oz/¼ cup) olive oil
1 bay leaf
5 garlic cloves, crushed
170 ml (5½ fl oz/⅔ cup) red wine
    vinegar
625 ml (21½ fl oz/2½ cups) beef stock
chopped flat-leaf (Italian) parsley,
    to garnish

Combine the flour with the cayenne pepper and season well. Lightly coat the veal with the flour, shaking off any excess.

Heat the oil in a large, deep frying pan over high heat and cook the veal, a few pieces at a time, for 1 minute each side, or until lightly browned. Remove from the pan and set aside.

Add the bay leaf, garlic, red wine vinegar and stock to the pan and bring to the boil, scraping up any residue from the base of the pan. Reduce the heat to low and return the veal and any juices back to the pan. Cover and cook, stirring gently occasionally, for 1½ hours, or until the veal is very tender and the sauce has thickened. If the sauce is too watery, carefully transfer the veal to a serving platter and boil the sauce until it is the consistency of a smooth gravy. Sprinkle with parsley before serving.

Roast Lamb with Lemon and Potatoes

⚜ SERVES 6
⚜ PREPARATION TIME: 20 MINUTES
⚜ COOKING TIME: 3 HOURS

2.5–3 kg (5 lb 8 oz–6 lb 12 oz) leg of
    lamb
2 garlic cloves, thinly sliced
125 ml (4 fl oz/½ cup) lemon juice
3 tablespoons dried oregano
1 onion, sliced
2 celery stalks, sliced
40 g (1½ oz) butter, softened
1 kg (2 lb 4 oz) all-purpose potatoes,
    quartered

Preheat the oven to 180°C (350°F/Gas 4). Cut small slits in the lamb. Insert the garlic into the slits. Rub the entire surface with half the lemon juice, sprinkle with salt, pepper and half the oregano. Place in a roasting tin and roast for 1 hour.

Drain the fat from the pan. Add the onion, celery and 250 ml (9 fl oz/1 cup) hot water. Spread the butter over the lamb, reduce the oven to 160°C (315°F/Gas 2–3) and cook for 1 hour. Turn during cooking to brown evenly.

Add the potatoes to the pan, sprinkle with the remaining oregano, lemon juice and some salt and pepper. Bake for another hour, adding more water if required and turning the potatoes halfway through cooking. Cut the lamb into slices. Skim any excess fat from the pan and serve the juices with the potatoes and lamb.

Veal Cooked with Vinegar

Thai Musaman Beef Curry

✻ SERVES 4
✻ PREPARATION TIME: 30 MINUTES
✻ COOKING TIME: 2 HOURS

1 tablespoon tamarind pulp
2 tablespoons vegetable oil
750 g (1 lb 10 oz) lean stewing beef,
    cubed
500 ml (17 fl oz/2 cups) coconut milk
4 cardamom pods, bruised
500 ml (17 fl oz/2 cups) coconut cream
2 tablespoons ready-made Musaman curry
    paste
2 tablespoons fish sauce
8 pickling onions (see Notes)
8 baby potatoes (see Notes)
2 tablespoons grated palm sugar (jaggery)
80 g (2¾ oz/½ cup) unsalted peanuts,
    roasted and ground

Put the tamarind pulp and 125 ml (4 fl oz/½ cup) boiling water in a bowl and set aside to cool. Mash the pulp with your fingertips to dissolve it, then strain and reserve the liquid, and discard the pulp.

Heat a non-stick wok over high heat, add the oil and swirl to coat the base and side. Add the beef in batches and cook over high heat for 5 minutes, or until browned all over. Reduce the heat, add the coconut milk and cardamom pods, and simmer for 1 hour, or until the beef is tender. Remove the beef from the wok. Strain the cooking liquid into a bowl and reserve.

Heat the coconut cream in the cleaned wok and stir in the curry paste. Cook for 10 minutes, or until the oil starts to separate from the cream. Add the fish sauce, onions, potatoes, beef mixture, palm sugar, peanuts, tamarind water and the reserved cooking liquid. Simmer for about 30 minutes, or until the sauce has thickened and the meat is tender.

NOTES: It is important that the pickling onions and baby potatoes are small and similar in size to ensure that they cook evenly.
    Also, use a non-stick or stainless steel wok as the tamarind purée will react with the metal in a regular wok and badly taint the dish.

Pork Chops in Marsala

※ SERVES 4
※ PREPARATION TIME: 10 MINUTES
※ COOKING TIME: 15 MINUTES

4 pork loin chops
2 tablespoons olive oil
125 ml (4 fl oz/½ cup) Marsala
2 teaspoons grated orange zest
60 ml (2 fl oz/¼ cup) orange juice
3 tablespoons chopped flat-leaf (Italian)
    parsley

Pat dry the chops and season well. Heat the olive oil in a heavy-based frying pan over medium heat and cook the chops on both sides for 5 minutes each side, or until brown and cooked. Add the Marsala, orange zest and juice and cook for 4–5 minutes, or until the sauce has reduced and thickened. Add the parsley and serve.

Shepherd's Pie

※ SERVES 6
※ PREPARATION TIME: 30 MINUTES
※ COOKING TIME: 1 HOUR 15 MINUTES

25 g (1 oz) butter
2 onions, finely chopped
30 g (1 oz/¼ cup) plain (all-purpose)
    flour
½ teaspoon dry mustard
375 ml (13 fl oz/1½ cups) chicken stock
750 g (1 lb 10 oz) lean cooked roast lamb,
    trimmed of excess fat and finely
    chopped
2 tablespoons worcestershire sauce
4 large all-purpose potatoes
125 ml (4 fl oz/½ cup) hot milk
30 g (1 oz) butter, extra

Lightly grease a 2 litre (70 fl oz/8-cup) casserole dish. Preheat the oven to 210°C (415°F/Gas 6–7). Melt the butter in a large frying pan, add the onion and stir over medium heat for 5–10 minutes, or until golden. Add the flour and mustard to the pan and cook for 1 minute, or until pale and foaming. Remove from the heat and gradually stir in the stock. Return to the heat and stir until the sauce boils and thickens. Reduce the heat and simmer for 2 minutes. Add the meat and worcestershire sauce and stir. Season to taste. Remove from the heat and spoon into the casserole dish.

Steam or boil the potatoes for 10–15 minutes, or until just tender. Drain and mash well. Add the milk and butter to the mashed potato, season and mix until smooth and creamy. Spread evenly over the meat and rough up the surface with the back of a spoon. Bake for 40–45 minutes, or until the meat is heated through and the topping is golden.

Pork Chops in Marsala

Game Pie

❊ SERVES 6–8

❊ PREPARATION TIME: 40 MINUTES

❊ COOKING TIME: 2 HOURS 30 MINUTES

1 kg (2 lb 4 oz) rabbit, boned, cut into
  bite-sized pieces

1.25 kg (2 lb 12 oz) diced venison

30 g (1 oz/¼ cup) plain (all-purpose)
  flour

2–3 tablespoons olive oil

2 bacon slices, chopped

1 onion, sliced into thin wedges

2 garlic cloves, crushed

150 g (5½ oz) button mushrooms, cut in
  halves

250 ml (9 fl oz/1 cup) red wine

250 ml (9 fl oz/1 cup) beef stock

3 thyme sprigs

2 bay leaves

185 g (6½ oz) ready-made puff pastry,
  thawed

1 egg yolk

2 tablespoons milk

Lightly coat the rabbit and venison in seasoned flour. Heat the oil in a large saucepan and cook the bacon over medium heat until golden. Remove. Brown the meat well in batches, remove and set aside. Add the onion and garlic to the pan and cook until browned.

Return the bacon and meat to the pan and add the mushrooms, wine, stock, thyme and bay leaves. Bring to the boil, then reduce the heat and simmer over low heat, stirring occasionally, for 1½ hours, or until the meat is tender. Transfer to a heatproof bowl. Remove the thyme and bay leaves. Refrigerate until cold.

Preheat the oven to 200°C (400°F/Gas 6). Spoon the mixture into a 2 litre (70 fl oz/8-cup) ovenproof dish. Roll out half the pastry on a lightly floured surface to about 5 mm (¼ inch) thick. Cut strips the width of the pie dish rim and secure to the dish with a little water. Reserve the leftover pastry. Roll out the other half of the pastry on a lightly floured surface until large enough to fit the top of the pie dish. Brush the edges of the pastry strips with a little combined egg yolk and milk. Drape the pastry over the rolling pin and lower it onto the top of the pie. Trim off any excess pastry using a sharp knife. Score the edges of the pastry with the back of a knife to seal. Use the leftover pastry to decorate the top. Cut two slits in the top of the pastry and brush all over with the remaining egg and milk mixture. Bake for 30–40 minutes, or until puffed and golden.

NOTES: Ask the butcher to bone the rabbit. Order the venison from the butcher.

Ramen Noodle Soup with Barbecued Pork and Greens

❀ SERVES 4

❀ PREPARATION TIME: 15 MINUTES

❀ COOKING TIME: 10 MINUTES

15 g (½ oz) dried shiitake mushrooms

125 ml (4 fl oz/½ cup) boiling water

350 g (12 oz) Chinese broccoli (gai larn), trimmed and cut into 4 cm (1½ inch) lengths

375 g (13 oz) fresh ramen noodles

1.25 litres (44 fl oz/5 cups) chicken stock

60 ml (2 fl oz/¼ cup) soy sauce

1 teaspoon sugar

200 g (7 oz) Chinese barbecued pork (char siu), thinly sliced

chilli flakes (optional)

Soak the mushrooms in the boiling water for 20 minutes. Squeeze the mushrooms dry, reserving the liquid. Discard the stalks, then thinly slice the caps. Set aside.

Blanch the Chinese broccoli in a large saucepan of boiling salted water for 3 minutes, or until tender but firm to the bite. Drain, then refresh in cold water. Set aside.

Cook the noodles in a large saucepan of boiling water for 2 minutes, or until just tender. Drain, rinse under cold water then drain again. Set aside.

Pour the stock and 500 ml (17 fl oz/2 cups) water into a non-stick wok and bring to the boil. Add the sliced mushrooms and reserved mushroom liquid, soy sauce and sugar. Simmer for 2 minutes, then add the broccoli.

Divide the noodles among four serving bowls. Ladle on the hot stock and vegetables. Top with the pork and chilli flakes, if desired.

Mexican Beef Chilli with Beans and Rice

❄ SERVES 4–6
❄ PREPARATION TIME: 20 MINUTES
❄ COOKING TIME: 2 HOURS

400 g (14 oz/2 cups) long-grain white
   rice
2 tablespoons olive oil
600 g (1 lb 5 oz) chuck steak, cut into
   2 cm (³/₄ inch) cubes
1 red onion, chopped
3 garlic cloves, crushed
1 long green chilli, finely chopped
2¹/₂ teaspoons ground cumin
2 teaspoons ground coriander
1 teaspoon chilli powder
3 teaspoons dried oregano
400 g (14 oz) tinned chopped tomatoes
2 tablespoons tomato paste (concentrated
   purée)
750 ml (26 fl oz/3 cups) beef stock
400 g (14 oz) tinned kidney beans,
   drained and rinsed
2 tablespoons oregano, chopped
burritos, to serve
sour cream, to serve

Put the rice in a heatproof bowl, add enough boiling water to cover and leave to soak until cool.

Meanwhile, heat 1 tablespoon of the oil in a large, heavy-based saucepan. Cook the beef in two batches until browned, then remove from the pan.

Heat the remaining oil in the pan and cook the onion for 2 minutes, or until softened but not browned. Add the garlic and chilli and cook for a further minute, then add the cumin, coriander, chilli powder and dried oregano and cook for a further 30 seconds. Return the beef to the pan and add the chopped tomatoes, tomato paste and 250 ml (9 fl oz/1 cup) of the stock. Bring to the boil, then reduce the heat and simmer, covered, for 1¹/₂ hours, or until the beef is tender.

Drain the rice and stir it into the beef mixture along with the kidney beans and remaining stock. Bring the mixture to the boil, then reduce the heat and simmer, covered, for 20 minutes, or until the rice is tender and all the liquid has been absorbed. Stir in the oregano and serve with warmed burritos and a dollop of sour cream. Let your guests assemble their own burritos at the table.

Rack of Lamb with Herb Crust

※ SERVES 4
※ PREPARATION TIME: 25 MINUTES
※ COOKING TIME: 25 MINUTES

2 x 6–rib racks of lamb, French-trimmed
1 tablespoon olive oil
80 g (2¾ oz/1 cup) fresh breadcrumbs
3 garlic cloves, finely chopped
3 tablespoons finely chopped flat-leaf
   (Italian) parsley
2 teapoons thyme leaves
½ teaspoon finely grated lemon zest
60 g (2¼ oz) butter, softened

JUS
250 ml (9 fl oz/1 cup) beef stock
1 garlic clove, finely chopped
1 thyme sprig

Preheat the oven to 250°C (500°F/Gas 9). Score the fat on the lamb racks in a diamond pattern. Rub with a little oil and season.

Heat the oil in a frying pan over high heat, add the lamb racks and brown for 4–5 minutes. Remove and set aside. Do not wash the pan as you will need it later.

In a large bowl, mix the breadcrumbs, garlic, parsley, thyme leaves and lemon zest. Season, then mix in the butter to form a paste.

Firmly press a layer of breadcrumb mixture over the fat on the lamb racks, leaving the bones and base clean. Bake in a roasting tin for 12 minutes for medium–rare. Rest the lamb on a plate while you make the jus.

To make the jus, add the beef stock, garlic and thyme to the roasting tin juices, scraping the pan. Return this liquid to the original frying pan and simmer over high heat for 5–8 minutes, or until the sauce has reduced. Strain and serve with the lamb.

Harira

❀ SERVES 4

❀ PREPARATION TIME: 15 MINUTES

❀ COOKING TIME: 2 HOURS 25 MINUTES

2 tablespoons olive oil

2 small brown onions, chopped

2 large garlic cloves, crushed

500 g (1 lb 2 oz) lamb shoulder steaks, trimmed of excess fat and sinew, and cut into small chunks

1½ teaspoons ground cumin

2 teaspoons paprika

½ teaspoon ground cloves

1 bay leaf

2 tablespoons tomato paste (concentrated purée)

1 litre (35 fl oz/4 cups) beef stock

900 g (2 lb) tinned chickpeas, rinsed and drained

800 g (1 lb 12 oz) tinned diced tomatoes

30 g (1 oz) finely chopped coriander (cilantro) leaves

coriander (cilantro) leaves, to garnish

small black olives (such as niçoise or Ligurian), to serve

Heat the oil in a large heavy-based saucepan or stockpot, add the onion and garlic and cook for 5 minutes, or until softened. Add the meat in batches and cook over high heat until browned on all sides. Return all the meat to the pan.

Add the spices and bay leaf to the pan and cook until fragrant. Add the tomato paste and cook for about 2 minutes, stirring constantly. Add the stock, stir well and bring to the boil. Add the chickpeas, tomato and the chopped coriander to the pan. Stir, then bring to the boil. Reduce the heat and simmer for 2 hours, or until the meat is tender. Stir occasionally. Season to taste.

Serve garnished with coriander leaves and olives. This dish can also be served with toasted pitta bread drizzled with a little extra virgin olive oil.

Beef Pho

❀ SERVES 4
❀ PREPARATION TIME: 15 MINUTES
❀ COOKING TIME: 35 MINUTES

2 litres (70 fl oz/8 cups) beef stock
1 star anise
4 cm (1½ inch) piece fresh ginger, sliced
2 pigs' trotters (cut in half)
½ onion, studded with 2 whole cloves
2 lemongrass stems, bruised
2 garlic cloves, crushed
¼ teaspoon ground white pepper
1 tablespoon fish sauce, plus extra, to serve
200 g (7 oz) fresh thin rice noodles
300 g (10½ oz) beef fillet, partially
    frozen, thinly sliced
90 g (3¼ oz/1 cup) bean sprouts,
    trimmed
2 spring onions (scallions), thinly sliced,
25 g (1 oz) chopped coriander (cilantro)
    leaves, plus extra, to serve
4 tablespoons chopped Vietnamese mint,
    plus extra, to serve
1 red chilli, thinly sliced, plus extra, to serve
2 limes, quartered

Put the beef stock, star anise, ginger, pigs' trotters, onion, lemongrass, garlic and white pepper in a wok and bring to the boil. Reduce the heat to very low and simmer, covered, for 30 minutes. Strain, return to the wok and stir in the fish sauce.

Meanwhile, put the noodles in a heatproof bowl, cover with boiling water and gently separate. Drain well then refresh under cold running water. Divide the noodles among four deep soup bowls, then top with beef strips, bean sprouts, spring onion, coriander, mint and chilli. Ladle over the broth.

Place the extra chilli, mint and coriander, the lime quarters and fish sauce in small bowls on a platter, serve with the soup and allow guests to help themselves.

Roman Lamb

※ SERVES 4–6
※ PREPARATION TIME: 15 MINUTES
※ COOKING TIME: 1 HOUR 20 MINUTES

60 ml (2 fl oz/¼ cup) olive oil
1 kg (2 lb 4 oz) spring lamb, cut into 2 cm
    (¾ inch) cubes
2 garlic cloves, crushed
6 sage leaves
1 rosemary sprig
1 tablespoon plain (all-purpose) flour
125 ml (4 fl oz/½ cup) white wine
    vinegar
6 anchovy fillets

Heat the oil in a heavy-based frying pan and cook the meat in batches over medium heat for 3–4 minutes, until browned on all sides. Return all the meat to the pan and add the garlic, sage and rosemary. Season, combine well and cook for 1 minute.

Dust the meat with the flour using a fine sieve, then cook for a further 1 minute. Add the vinegar and simmer for 30 seconds, then add 250 ml (9 fl oz/ 1 cup) water. Bring to a gentle simmer, lower the heat and cover, leaving the lid partially askew. Cook for 50–60 minutes, or until the meat is tender, stirring occasionally and adding a little more water if necessary.

When the lamb is almost cooked, mash the anchovies and 1 tablespoon of the cooking liquid to a paste using a mortar and pestle. Add to the lamb and cook, uncovered, for another 2 minutes.

Chilli Plum Beef

※ SERVES 4
※ PREPARATION TIME: 15 MINUTES
※ COOKING TIME: 15 MINUTES

2 tablespoons vegetable oil
600 g (1 lb 5 oz) lean beef fillet, thinly
    sliced across the grain
1 large red onion, cut into wedges
1 red capsicum (pepper), seeded,
    membrane removed and finely sliced
1½ tablespoons chilli garlic sauce
125 ml (4 fl oz/½ cup) plum sauce
1 tablespoon light soy sauce
2 teaspoons rice vinegar
pinch finely ground white pepper
4 spring onions (scallions), sliced
steamed rice or noodles, to serve

Heat a wok over high heat, add 1 tablespoon of the oil and swirl to coat the base and side. Stir-fry the beef in two batches for 2–3 minutes, or until browned and just cooked. Remove from the wok and set aside.

Heat the remaining oil in the wok, add the onion and stir-fry for 1 minute, then add the capsicum and stir-fry for 2–3 minutes, or until just tender. Add the chilli garlic sauce and stir for 1 minute, then return the meat to the wok and add the plum sauce, soy sauce, vinegar, white pepper and most of the spring onion.

Toss everything together for 1 minute, or until the meat is heated through. Sprinkle with the remaining spring onion and serve with steamed rice or noodles.

Roman Lamb

Rigatoni with Italian-style Oxtail Sauce

✼ SERVES 4

✼ PREPARATION TIME: 25 MINUTES

✼ COOKING TIME: 2 HOURS

2 tablespoons olive oil

1.5 kg (3 lb 5 oz) oxtail, jointed

2 large onions, sliced

4 garlic cloves, chopped

2 celery stalks, sliced

2 carrots, thinly sliced

2 large rosemary sprigs

60 ml (2 fl oz/¼ cup) red wine

60 ml (2 fl oz/¼ cup) tomato paste
    (concentrated purée)

4 tomatoes, peeled and chopped

1.5 litres (52 fl oz/6 cups) beef stock

500 g (1 lb 2 oz) rigatoni

Heat the oil in a large heavy-based saucepan. Brown the oxtail, remove from the pan and set aside. Add the onion, garlic, celery and carrot to the pan and stir for 3–4 minutes, or until the onion is lightly browned.

Return the oxtail to the pan and add the rosemary and red wine. Cover and cook for 10 minutes, shaking the pan occasionally to prevent the meat from sticking to the bottom. Add the tomato paste and tomato to the pan with 500 ml (17 fl oz/2 cups) of the beef stock and simmer, uncovered, for 30 minutes, stirring the mixture occasionally.

Add another 500 ml (17 fl oz/2 cups) of beef stock to the pan and cook for 30 minutes. Add 250 ml (9 fl oz/1 cup) of stock and cook for 30 minutes. Finally, add the remaining stock and cook until the oxtail is tender and the meat is falling from the bone. The liquid should have reduced to produce a thick sauce.

Just before the meat is cooked, cook the pasta in a large saucepan of rapidly boiling salted water until *al dente*. Serve the meat and sauce over the hot pasta.

NOTE: For a different flavour, you can add 250 g (9 oz) bacon to the cooked onion, garlic and vegetables.

Beef Wellington

* SERVES 6–8
* PREPARATION TIME: 25 MINUTES
* COOKING TIME: 1 HOUR 30 MINUTES

1.25 kg (2 lb 12 oz) beef fillet or rib-eye
   in 1 piece
1 tablespoon olive oil
125 g (4½ oz) pâté
60 g (2¼ oz) button mushrooms, sliced
375 g (13 oz) block ready-made puff
   pastry, thawed
1 egg, lightly beaten
1 sheet ready-rolled puff pastry, thawed

Preheat the oven to 210°C (415°F/Gas 6–7). Trim the meat of any excess fat and sinew. Fold the thinner part of the tail end under the meat and tie securely with kitchen string at regular intervals to form an even shape.

Rub the meat with freshly ground black pepper. Heat the oil over high heat in a large frying pan. Add the meat and brown well all over. Remove from the heat and allow to cool. Remove the string.

Spread the pâté over the top and sides of the beef. Cover with the mushrooms, pressing them onto the pâté. Roll out the block pastry on a lightly floured surface to a rectangle large enough to completely enclose the beef.

Place the beef on the pastry, brush the edges with the egg, and fold over to enclose the meat completely. Brush the edges of the pastry with egg to seal, and fold in the ends. Invert onto a greased baking tray so the seam is underneath. Cut leaf shapes from the sheet of puff pastry and use to decorate the Wellington. Use the egg to stick on the shapes. Cut a few slits in the top to allow the steam to escape. Brush the top and the sides of the pastry with the egg, and cook for 45 minutes for rare, 1 hour for medium or 1 hour 30 minutes for well done. Leave in a warm place for 10 minutes before cutting into slices for serving.

NOTE: Use a firm pâté, discarding any jelly. Cover the pastry loosely with foil if it begins to darken too much during cooking.

Stuffed Leg of Lamb

🌿 SERVES 6–8

🌿 PREPARATION TIME: 25 MINUTES

🌿 COOKING TIME: 2 HOURS 15 MINUTES

STUFFING

1 thick slice white bread, crusts removed
70 g (2 1/2 oz) chicken livers, trimmed
60 g (2 1/4 oz) bacon or tocino
1 tablespoon dry sherry
1 garlic clove, crushed
1 tablespoon chopped flat-leaf (Italian) parsley
1/2 tablespoon snipped chives
1 teaspoon finely chopped rosemary
1 tablespoon capers, finely chopped

1 large leg of lamb (3 kg/6 lb 12 oz), boned
1 teaspoon sweet paprika
1 tablespoon plain (all-purpose) flour
4 garlic cloves, peeled
2 tablespoons olive oil
375 ml (13 fl oz/1 1/2 cups) dry white wine
1 tablespoon lard
125 ml (4 fl oz/1/2 cup) chicken stock

To make the stuffing, break the bread into pieces and process with the chicken livers and bacon until medium-fine. Put in a bowl with the sherry, garlic, parsley, chives, rosemary and capers. Season and mix well.

Preheat the oven to 210°C (415°F/Gas 6–7). Lay the lamb out flat and put the filling down the centre. Roll the meat up to encase the filling. Tie with kitchen string. Combine the paprika and flour with 1/4 teaspoon salt and rub all over the lamb. Put the garlic in a row in the centre of a baking dish and pour the oil over the top. Put the lamb on the garlic and pour the wine over the top. Spread the lard over the top of the lamb.

Bake for 20 minutes, then reduce the heat to 170°C (325°F/Gas 3). Baste, then bake for a further 1 hour 45 minutes, basting frequently, until the lamb is well cooked. Transfer the lamb to a carving tray and keep warm. Spoon off excess oil from the pan juices, then transfer the contents of the baking dish to a saucepan. Add the stock and cook over high heat until slightly thickened. Slice the lamb and arrange on a serving platter. Pour the sauce over the lamb.

Meatballs

🌿 MAKES ABOUT 25

🌿 PREPARATION TIME: 25 MINUTES

🌿 COOKING TIME: 20 MINUTES

250 g (9 oz) minced (ground) lean beef
1 small onion, grated
1 garlic clove, crushed
40 g (1 1/2 oz/1/2 cup) fresh white breadcrumbs
40 g (1 1/2 oz/1/3 cup) pitted black olives,
   chopped
1 teaspoon dried oregano
1 tablespoon finely chopped flat-leaf (Italian)
   parsley
olive oil, for pan-frying

Combine the beef, onion, garlic, breadcrumbs, olives, oregano, parsley and salt and black pepper, to taste. Mix together thoroughly.

Form teaspoons of the mixture into balls. This is easier if you roll them with wet hands. Heat a little oil in a frying pan and cook the meatballs in batches until well browned and cooked through.

NOTE: You can prepare the meatballs and cover and refrigerate them until you are ready to cook. Or, you can cook them in advance and reheat them, lightly covered with foil, in a 160°C (315°F/Gas 2–3) oven. They can also be cooked and frozen, then reheated.

Stuffed Leg of Lamb

Parmesan and Rosemary Crusted Veal Chops

❀ SERVES 4

❀ PREPARATION TIME: 15 MINUTES

❀ COOKING TIME: 15 MINUTES

4 veal chops
150 g (5½ oz) fresh white breadcrumbs
75 g (2¾ oz/¾ cup) freshly grated
    parmesan cheese
1 tablespoon rosemary, finely chopped
2 eggs, lightly beaten, seasoned
60 ml (2 fl oz/¼ cup) olive oil
60 g (2¼ oz) butter
4 garlic cloves, peeled

Trim the chops of excess fat and sinew and flatten to 1 cm (½ inch) thickness. Pat the meat dry with paper towels. Combine the breadcrumbs, parmesan and rosemary in a shallow bowl.

Dip each chop in the beaten egg, draining off the excess. Press both sides of the chops firmly in the crumbs.

Heat the oil and butter in a heavy-based frying pan over low heat, add the garlic and cook until golden. Discard the garlic.

Increase the heat to medium, add the chops to the pan and cook for 4–5 minutes on each side, depending on the thickness of the chops, until golden and crisp. Transfer to a warm serving dish and season.

Spaghetti Bolognese

❀ SERVES 4–6

❀ PREPARATION TIME: 20 MINUTES

❀ COOKING TIME: 1 HOUR 40 MINUTES

2 tablespoons olive oil
2 garlic cloves, crushed
1 large onion, chopped
1 carrot, chopped
1 celery stalk, chopped
500 g (1 lb 2 oz) minced (ground) beef
500 ml (17 fl oz/2 cups) beef stock
375 ml (13 fl oz/1½ cups) red wine
850 g (1 lb 14 oz) tinned crushed
    tomatoes
1 teaspoon sugar
3 tablespoons chopped flat-leaf (Italian)
    parsley
500 g (1 lb 2 oz) spaghetti
freshly grated parmesan cheese, to serve

Heat the olive oil in a largem deep frying pan. Add the garlic, onion, carrot and celery and stir for 5 minutes over low heat until the vegetables are golden.

Increase the heat, add the beef and brown well, stirring and breaking up any lumps with a fork as it cooks. Add the stock, wine, tomato, sugar and parsley. Bring the mixture to the boil, then reduce the heat and simmer for 1 hour 30 minutes, stirring occasionally. Season.

While the sauce is cooking and shortly before serving, cook the pasta in a large saucepan of rapidly boiling salted water until *al dente*. Drain and then divide among serving bowls. Serve the sauce over the top of the pasta and sprinkle with the freshly grated parmesan cheese.

Parmesan and Rosemary Crusted Veal Chops

Steak and Kidney Pie

750 g (1 lb 10 oz) round steak, trimmed
    of excess fat and sinew
4 lamb kidneys
2 tablespoons plain (all-purpose) flour
1 tablespoon olive oil
1 onion, chopped
30 g (1 oz) butter
1 tablespoon worcestershire sauce
1 tablespoon tomato paste (concentrated
    purée)
125 ml (4 fl oz/½ cup) red wine
250 ml (9 fl oz/1 cup) beef stock
125 g (4½ oz) button mushrooms, sliced
½ teaspoon dried thyme
4 tablespoons chopped flat-leaf (Italian)
    parsley
500 g (1 lb 2 oz) block ready-made puff
    pastry, thawed
1 egg, lightly beaten

Cut the steak into 2 cm (¾ inch) cubes. Peel the skin from the kidneys, quarter them and trim away any fat or sinew. Put the flour in a plastic bag with the meat and kidneys and toss gently. Heat the oil in a frying pan, add the onion and fry for 5 minutes, or until soft. Remove from the pan with a slotted spoon. Add the butter to the pan, brown the steak and kidneys in batches and then return the steak, kidneys and onion to the pan.

Add the worcestershire sauce, tomato paste, wine, stock, mushrooms and herbs to the pan. Bring to the boil, reduce the heat and simmer, covered, for 1 hour, or until the meat is tender. Season to taste and allow to cool. Spoon into a 1.5 litre (52 fl oz/6-cup) pie dish.

Preheat the oven to 210°C (415°F/Gas 6–7). Roll out the pastry between two sheets of baking paper, to a size 4 cm (1½ inches) larger than the pie dish. Cut thin strips from the edge of the pastry and press onto the rim of the dish, sealing the joins. Place the pastry on the pie, trim the edges and cut two steam holes in the pastry. Decorate the pie with leftover pastry and brush the top with the egg. Bake for 35–40 minutes, or until the pastry is golden.

Veal Wrapped in Prosciutto with Honeyed Wild Rice

❀ SERVES 4

❀ PREPARATION TIME: 25 MINUTES

❀ COOKING TIME: 35 MINUTES

500 g (1 lb 2 oz/1 bunch) English
    spinach, stalks removed
4 veal steaks (200 g/7 oz each), slightly
    flattened
16 slices prosciutto
2 tablespoons wholegrain mustard

HONEYED WILD RICE
210 g (7½ oz/1 cup) wild rice blend
30 g (1 oz) butter
1 onion, finely chopped
1 garlic clove, crushed
1 tablespoon honey
1 tablespoon light soy sauce

2 tablespoons olive oil
2 garlic cloves, crushed
125 ml (4 fl oz/½ cup) dry white wine
250 ml (9 fl oz/1 cup) chicken stock
1 tablespoon dijon mustard
1 teaspoon cornflour (cornstarch),
    blended with 2 tablespoons cold water
1 tablespoon chervil sprigs

Preheat the oven to 180°C (350°F/Gas 4). Steam the spinach until just wilted, then rinse in cold water, drain and pat dry. Put a few spinach leaves on a cutting board to form a square, a little larger than a veal steak. Also on the board, lay out four prosciutto slices, slightly overlapping, with the short ends towards you. Put a steak on the spinach square, spread it with a quarter of the wholegrain mustard and roll up both the veal and spinach to form a log. Lay the veal and spinach log across the bottom edge of the pieces of prosciutto and roll up, folding in the sides as you go, to form a parcel. Repeat with the remaining spinach, veal, wholegrain mustard and prosciutto until you end up with four parcels.

To make the honeyed wild rice, bring a large saucepan of water to the boil. Add the rice and cook, stirring occasionally, for 25 minutes, or until tender, then drain. Heat the butter in a small frying pan, add the onion and garlic and cook until the onion is softened but not browned. Add the rice, honey and soy sauce, toss thoroughly, then remove from the heat.

Meanwhile, heat the oil in a frying pan over medium heat and cook the veal parcels until lightly browned, turning frequently. Remove from the pan and transfer to a roasting tin. Bake for 10–15 minutes. Remove from the oven, cover and keep warm.

Put the roasting tin on the stovetop over medium heat, add the garlic and wine and cook for 2 minutes. Add the stock, dijon mustard and cornflour paste. Stir until the sauce boils and thickens. Strain. Slice the veal thickly, pour over the sauce and sprinkle with the chervil.

Saltimbocca

❧ SERVES 4
❧ PREPARATION TIME: 15 MINUTES
❧ COOKING TIME: 20 MINUTES

4 thin veal steaks
2 garlic cloves, crushed
4 prosciutto slices
4 sage leaves
30 g (1 oz) butter
170 ml (5½ fl oz/⅔ cup) Marsala

Trim the meat of excess fat and sinew and flatten each steak to 5 mm (¼ inch) thick. Nick the edges to prevent curling and pat the meat dry with paper towels. Combine the garlic with ¼ teaspoon salt and ½ teaspoon ground black pepper and rub some of the mixture over one side of each veal steak. Place a slice of prosciutto on each and top with a sage leaf. The prosciutto should cover the veal completely but not overlap the edge.

Melt the butter in a large heavy-based frying pan, add the veal, prosciutto side up, and cook over medium–high heat for 5 minutes, or until the underside is golden brown. Do not turn the veal. Add the Marsala, without wetting the top of the veal. Reduce the heat and simmer very slowly for 10 minutes. Transfer the veal to warm serving plates. Boil the sauce for 2–3 minutes, or until syrupy, then spoon it over the veal.

Braised Lamb Shanks with Haricot Beans

❧ SERVES 4
❧ PREPARATION TIME: 10 MINUTES
❧ COOKING TIME: 2 HOURS 15 MINUTES

400 g (14 oz/2 cups) dried haricot beans
80 ml (2½ fl oz/⅓ cup) olive oil
4 lamb shanks, trimmed
40 g (1½ oz) butter
2 garlic cloves, crushed
2 onions, finely chopped
1½ tablespoons thyme
2 tablespoons tomato paste (concentrated purée)
800 g (1 lb 12 oz) tinned crushed tomatoes
1 tablespoon paprika
1 dried jalapeño chilli, roughly chopped
30 g (1 oz) roughly chopped flat-leaf (Italian) parsley

Put the beans in a bowl, cover with water and soak overnight. In a large heavy-based saucepan, heat 3 tablespoons of the oil over medium heat and brown the lamb on all sides. Remove, then set aside and drain the fat from the pan. Heat the butter and remaining oil in the pan and cook the garlic and onion over medium heat for 3–4 minutes, or until softened. Add the thyme, tomato paste, tomato and paprika and simmer for 5 minutes. Add the lamb shanks and 500 ml (17 fl oz/ 2 cups) hot water. Season and bring to the boil. Cover, reduce the heat and simmer gently for 30 minutes.

Drain the beans and add to the pan with the chilli and another 500 ml (17 fl oz/2 cups) hot water. Bring to the boil, cover and simmer for another 1 hour–1 hour 30 minutes, or until the beans and the meat are tender, adding more water, 125 ml (4 fl oz/½ cup) at a time, if necessary. Adjust the seasoning and stir in half the parsley. Serve hot, sprinkled with the remaining parsley.

Saltimbocca

Shish Kebabs with Capsicum and Herbs

1 kg (2 lb 4 oz) boneless leg of lamb
1 red capsicum (pepper)
1 green capsicum (pepper)
3 red onions
olive oil, for brushing

MARINADE
1 onion, thinly sliced
2 garlic cloves, crushed
60 ml (2 fl oz/ $\frac{1}{4}$ cup) lemon juice
80 ml (2 $\frac{1}{2}$ fl oz/ $\frac{1}{3}$ cup) olive oil
1 tablespoon chopped thyme
1 tablespoon paprika
$\frac{1}{2}$ teaspoon chilli flakes
2 teaspoons ground cumin
15 g ($\frac{1}{2}$ oz) chopped flat-leaf (Italian)
   parsley
20 g ($\frac{3}{4}$ oz) chopped mint

If using wooden skewers, soak in water for about 30 minutes to prevent them from burning during cooking.

Trim the sinew and most of the fat from the lamb and cut the meat into 3 cm (1 $\frac{1}{4}$ inch) cubes. Mix all the ingredients for the marinade in a large bowl. Season, add the meat and mix well. Cover and refrigerate for 4–6 hours, or overnight.

Remove the seeds and membrane from the capsicums and cut the flesh into 3 cm (1 $\frac{1}{4}$ inch) squares. Cut each red onion into six wedges. Remove the lamb from the marinade and reserve the liquid. Thread the meat onto the skewers, alternating with onion and capsicum pieces. Grill (broil) the skewers for 5–6 minutes, brushing frequently with the marinade for the first couple of minutes. Serve immediately. These are delicious served with bread or pilaff.

Pasticcio

❀ SERVES 6
❀ PREPARATION TIME: 1 HOUR
❀ COOKING TIME: 1 HOUR 50 MINUTES

250 g (9 oz/2 cups) plain (all-purpose)
　　flour
125 g (4½ oz) cold butter, chopped
55 g (2 oz/¼ cup) caster (superfine)
　　sugar
1 egg yolk
150 g (5½ oz) bucatini or penne

FILLING
2 tablespoons olive oil
1 onion, chopped
2 garlic cloves, finely chopped
500 g (1 lb 2 oz) minced (ground) beef
150 g (5½ oz) chicken livers
2 tomatoes, chopped
125 ml (4 fl oz/½ cup) red wine
125 ml (4 fl oz/½ cup) rich beef stock
1 tablespoon chopped oregano
¼ teaspoon freshly grated nutmeg
50 g (1¾ oz/½ cup) freshly grated
　　parmesan cheese

BÉCHAMEL SAUCE
60 g (2¼ oz) butter
2 tablespoons plain (all-purpose) flour
375 ml (12 fl oz/1½ cups) cold milk

Put the flour, butter, sugar and egg yolk in a food processor with 1 tablespoon water. Process lightly until the mixture forms a ball, adding more water if necessary. Lightly knead the dough on a floured surface until smooth. Wrap in plastic wrap and refrigerate.

To make the filling, heat the oil in a heavy-based saucepan and cook the onion and garlic until softened and lightly golden. Increase the heat, add the beef and cook until browned, breaking up any lumps with a fork. Add the livers, tomato, red wine, stock, oregano and nutmeg, then season well. Cook the sauce over high heat until it boils, reduce to a simmer and cook, covered, for 40 minutes, then cool. Stir in the parmesan.

To make the béchamel sauce, heat the butter in a saucepan over low heat. Add the flour and stir for 1 minute, or until the mixture is golden and smooth. Remove from the heat and gradually stir in the milk. Return to the heat and stir constantly until the sauce boils and begins to thicken. Simmer for another minute. Season to taste.

Cook the bucatini in a saucepan of rapidly boiling salted water until *al dente*. Drain and cool.

Preheat the oven to 160°C (315°F/Gas 2–3). Lightly grease a deep 23 cm (9 inch) pie dish. Divide the dough into two and roll out one piece to fit the base of the prepared dish, allowing the edges to overhang the side. Spoon about half of the meat mixture into the dish, top with the bucatini and slowly spoon the béchamel sauce over the top, allowing it to seep down and coat the bucatini. Top with the remaining meat. Roll out the remaining dough and cover the pie. Trim the edges and pinch lightly to seal. Bake for 50–55 minutes, or until dark golden brown and crisp. Set aside for 15 minutes before cutting.

Osso Bucco alla Milanese

❋ SERVES 4
❋ PREPARATION TIME: 30 MINUTES
❋ COOKING TIME: 1 HOUR 40 MINUTES

12 pieces veal shank, about 4 cm
    (1½ inch) thick
plain (all-purpose) flour, seasoned, for
    dusting
60 ml (2 fl oz/¼ cup) olive oil
60 g (2¼ oz) butter
1 garlic clove, finely chopped
1 onion, finely chopped
1 celery stalk, finely chopped
250 ml (9 fl oz/1 cup) dry white wine
1 bay leaf or lemon leaf
pinch ground allspice
pinch ground cinnamon

GREMOLATA
2 teaspoons finely grated lemon zest
2 tablespoons finely chopped flat-leaf
    (Italian) parsley
1 garlic clove, finely chopped

Dust each piece of veal shank with seasoned flour. Heat the oil, butter, garlic, onion and celery in a heavy-based frying pan or saucepan that is big enough to hold the shanks in a single layer (but don't add the shanks yet). Cook for about 5 minutes over low heat until softened but not browned. Add the shanks to the pan, increase heat to medium and cook for 12–15 minutes, or until well browned all over. Arrange the shanks in the pan, standing them up in a single layer. Pour in the wine and add the bay leaf, allspice and cinnamon. Bring to the boil and cover the pan. Turn the heat down to low.

Cook at a simmer for 15 minutes, then add 125 ml (4 fl oz/½ cup) warm water. Continue cooking, covered, for 45–60 minutes (the timing will depend on the age of the veal) or until the meat is tender and you can cut it with a fork. Check the volume of liquid once or twice during cooking time and add more warm water as needed.

To make the gremolata, mix together the lemon zest, parsley and garlic.

Transfer the veal shanks to a plate and keep warm. Discard the bay leaf. Increase the heat under the pan and stir for 1–2 minutes until the sauce has thickened, scraping up any bits off the bottom of the pan. Season to taste and return the veal shanks to the sauce. Heat everything through, then stir in half the gremolata. Serve sprinkled with the remaining gremolata.

Shanghai Pork Noodles

❀ SERVES 4
❀ PREPARATION TIME: 25 MINUTES
❀ COOKING TIME: 20 MINUTES

½ teaspoon sesame oil

60 ml (2 fl oz/¼ cup) soy sauce

2 tablespoons oyster sauce

250 g (9 oz) pork loin fillet, cut into very
    thin strips

2 tablespoons dried shrimp

8 dried shiitake mushrooms

1 teaspoon sugar

250 ml (9 fl oz/1 cup) chicken stock

300 g (10½ oz) fresh Shanghai noodles

2 tablespoons peanut oil

1 garlic clove, thinly sliced

2 teaspoons grated fresh ginger

1 celery stalk, cut into matchsticks

1 leek, white part only, cut into
    matchsticks

150 g (5½ oz) Chinese cabbage (wong
    bok), shredded

50 g (1¾ oz) tinned bamboo shoots, cut
    into matchsticks

8 spring onions (scallions), thinly sliced

Combine the sesame oil and 1 tablespoon each of the soy sauce and oyster sauce in a large non-metallic bowl. Add the pork strips and toss in the marinade. Cover and marinate in the refrigerator for 30 minutes.

Meanwhile, put the dried shrimp in a bowl, cover with boiling water and soak for 20 minutes. Drain and finely chop. At the same time, put the shiitake mushrooms in a heatproof bowl, cover with boiling water and soak for 20 minutes. Drain, squeeze the mushrooms dry, discard the stems and thinly slice the caps.

To make the stir-fry sauce, combine the sugar, stock, remaining soy and oyster sauces and 1 teaspoon salt in a small non-metallic bowl. Set aside.

Cook the noodles in a large saucepan of boiling water for 4–5 minutes, or until tender. Drain and refresh under cold water. Toss with 1 teaspoon of the peanut oil.

Heat a wok over high heat, add 1 tablespoon of the peanut oil and swirl to coat the base and side. Add the pork and stir-fry for 1–2 minutes, or until the pork is no longer pink. Transfer to a plate.

Heat the remaining peanut oil, add the garlic, ginger, celery, leek and cabbage and stir-fry for 1 minute, or until softened. Add the bamboo shoots, spring onion, shrimp and mushrooms and stir-fry for 1 minute. Add the noodles and the stir-fry sauce and toss together for 3–5 minutes, or until the noodles absorb the sauce.

Return the pork to the wok, with any juices, and toss for 1–2 minutes, or until combined and heated through. Serve immediately.

Lamb Braise with Eggplant Cream

❀ SERVES 6–8
❀ PREPARATION TIME: 30 MINUTES
❀ COOKING TIME: 1 HOUR 45 MINUTES

2 tablespoons olive oil
1 kg (2 lb 4 oz) lamb, cut into 2 cm
    (³⁄₄ inch) cubes
1 large onion, chopped
1 bay leaf
small pinch ground cloves
2 garlic cloves, crushed
2 tablespoons tomato paste (concentrated
    purée)
400 g (14 oz) tinned chopped tomatoes
30 g (1 oz) chopped flat-leaf (Italian)
    parsley
750 ml (26 fl oz/3 cups) beef stock
125 g (4¹⁄₂ oz) vine-ripened tomatoes,
    chopped
chopped flat-leaf (Italian) parsley, to
    garnish

EGGPLANT CREAM
1 kg (2 lb 4 oz) eggplants (aubergines)
60 g (2¹⁄₄ oz) butter
2¹⁄₂ tablespoons plain (all-purpose) flour
310 ml (10³⁄₄ fl oz/1¹⁄₄ cups) cream
60 g (2¹⁄₄ oz/²⁄₃ cup) grated kasseri cheese
    (see Note)
large pinch freshly grated nutmeg

Heat the oil in a large, deep saucepan over high heat and cook the lamb in three batches for 4–5 minutes, or until well browned. Remove the lamb from the pan with a slotted spoon and set aside.

Add the onion to the pan, cook for 5 minutes, or until golden, then add the bay leaf, cloves, garlic, tomato paste, tinned tomatoes, parsley, stock and lamb and stir well. Bring to the boil, then reduce the heat to low. Cover and simmer, stirring occasionally for about 1 hour 30 minutes, or until the lamb is very tender and the sauce is thick. Season to taste.

Meanwhile, to make the eggplant cream, preheat the oven to 200°C (400°F/Gas 6). Pierce the eggplants a few times with a fork and, using a long-handled fork, roast them over an open flame (either a gas stovetop or a barbecue) for about 5 minutes, turning occasionally, until blackened and blistered all over. This will give them a good smoky flavour. Place the eggplants on a baking tray and bake for about 30 minutes, or until the eggplants are shrivelled and the flesh is very soft. Transfer to a colander and leave to cool.

When cool, peel the eggplants, ensuring all the skin is removed and discarded. Chop the flesh and set aside. Melt the butter in a saucepan over medium heat and add the flour. Stir for 2 minutes, or until it has a toasty aroma and darkens slightly. Gradually pour in the cream, whisking until smooth, then stir in the eggplant. Add the cheese and nutmeg and stir until the cheese has melted. Season.

Spread the eggplant cream on a serving plate, place the lamb in the centre and sprinkle with the chopped tomato and parsley. Serve immediately.

NOTE: Kasseri cheese, available at specialist delicatessens, is a sheep or goat's milk cheese, often used on top of lamb stews.

Roast Sirloin with Mustard Sauce

❋ SERVES 6
❋ PREPARATION TIME: 15 MINUTES
❋ COOKING TIME: 1 HOUR 15 MINUTES

1.5 kg (3 lb 5 oz) beef sirloin
90 g (3¼ oz/⅓ cup) wholegrain mustard
1 tablespoon dijon mustard
1 teaspoon honey
1 garlic clove, crushed
1 tablespoon olive oil

MUSTARD SAUCE
250 ml (9 fl oz/1 cup) white wine
1 tablespoon dijon mustard
60 g (2¼ oz/¼ cup) wholegrain mustard
2 tablespoons honey
200 g (7 oz) chilled butter, cubed

Preheat the oven to 220°C (425°F/Gas 7). Cut most of the fat from the beef sirloin, leaving a thin layer. Mix together the mustards and add the honey and garlic. Spread over the sirloin in a thick layer. Place the oil in a baking dish and heat it in the oven for 2 minutes. Place the meat in the hot dish and roast for 15 minutes. Reduce the oven to 200°C (400°F/Gas 6) and cook for 45–50 minutes for medium–rare, or until cooked to your liking.

To make the sauce, pour the wine into a saucepan and cook over high heat for 5 minutes, or until reduced by half. Add the mustards and honey. Reduce the heat and whisk in the butter. Remove from the heat and season. Serve thin slices of the meat with the sauce and roast vegetables.

Lamb Crown Roast with Sage Stuffing

❋ SERVES 4–6
❋ PREPARATION TIME: 30 MINUTES
❋ COOKING TIME: 50 MINUTES

1 crown roast of lamb (12 cutlets)
20 g (¾ oz) butter
2 onions, chopped
1 green apple, peeled and chopped
160 g (5¾ oz/2 cups) fresh breadcrumbs
2 tablespoons chopped sage
1 tablespoon chopped flat-leaf (Italian)
    parsley
60 ml (2 fl oz/¼ cup) unsweetened apple
    juice
2 eggs, separated

Preheat the oven to 210°C (415°F/Gas 6–7). Trim the meat of excess fat and sinew.

Melt the butter in a saucepan. Add the onion and apple and cook over medium heat until soft. Remove from the heat and stir into the combined breadcrumbs, sage and parsley. Whisk the apple juice and egg yolks together, then stir into the breadcrumb mixture. Beat the egg whites using electric beaters until soft peaks form. Fold into the stuffing mixture.

Place the roast on a sheet of greased foil in a baking dish. Wrap some foil around the tops of the bones to prevent burning. Spoon the stuffing into the cavity. Roast for 45 minutes for medium, or until cooked to your liking. Leave for 10 minutes before cutting between the cutlets.

Roast Sirloin with Mustard Sauce

Tagliatelle with Veal, Wine and Cream

※ SERVES 4
※ PREPARATION TIME: 15 MINUTES
※ COOKING TIME: 20 MINUTES

500 g (1 lb 2 oz) veal scaloppine or
    escalopes, cut into thin strips
plain (all-purpose) flour, seasoned
60 g (2¼ oz) butter
1 onion, sliced
125 ml (4 fl oz/½ cup) dry white wine
60 ml (2 fl oz/¼ cup) beef stock or
    chicken stock
170 ml (5½ fl oz/⅔ cup) cream
600 g (1 lb 5 oz) fresh plain or spinach
    tagliatelle (or a mixture of both)
1 tablespoon freshly grated parmesan
    cheese, plus extra, to serve (optional)
flat-leaf (Italian) parsley, to garnish

Coat the veal strips with the seasoned flour. Melt the butter in a frying pan. Add the veal strips and fry quickly until browned. Remove with a slotted spoon and set aside.

Add the onion slices to the pan and stir until soft and golden. Pour in the wine and cook rapidly to reduce the liquid. Add the stock and cream. Season to taste. Reduce the sauce again, and add the veal towards the end.

Meanwhile, cook the tagliatelle in a large saucepan of rapidly boiling salted water until *al dente*. Drain and transfer to a warm serving dish.

Stir the parmesan through the sauce. Pour the sauce over the pasta. Serve with extra parmesan, if desired, and garnish with parsley.

Slow-Roasted Lamb with Cumin and Paprika

※ SERVES 6
※ PREPARATION TIME: 15 MINUTES
※ COOKING TIME: 3 HOURS 30 MINUTES

2.25 kg (5 lb) leg of lamb
80 g (2¾ oz) butter, softened
3 garlic cloves, crushed
2 teaspoons ground cumin
3 teaspoons ground coriander
1 teaspoon paprika
1 tablespoon ground cumin, extra,
    for dipping

Preheat the oven to 220°C (425°F/Gas 7). Cut small deep slits in the top and sides of the lamb.

Mix the butter, garlic, spices and ¼ teaspoon salt in a bowl until a smooth paste forms.

With the back of a spoon, rub the paste all over the lamb, then use your fingers to spread the paste and make sure all the lamb is covered.

Put the lamb, bone side down, in a deep roasting tin and place on the top shelf of the oven. Bake for 0 minutes, then baste and return to the oven. Reduce the temperature to 160°C (315°F/Gas 2–3). Bake for 3 hours 20 minutes, basting every 20–30 minutes to make the lamb tender and flavoursome. Carve the lamb into chunky slices. Mix the cumin with 1½ teaspoons salt and serve on the side for dipping.

Tagliatelle with Veal, Wine and Cream

Rabbit Casserole with Mustard Sauce

* SERVES 4–6
* PREPARATION TIME: 30 MINUTES
* COOKING TIME: 2 HOURS

2 rabbits (800 g/1 lb 12 oz each)
2 tablespoons olive oil
2 onions, sliced
4 bacon slices, cut into 3 cm (1 1/4 inch)
    pieces
2 tablespoons plain (all-purpose) flour
375 ml (13 fl oz/1 1/2 cups) chicken stock
125 ml (4 fl oz/1/2 cup) dry white wine
1 teaspoon thyme leaves
125 ml (4 fl oz/1/2 cup) cream
2 tablespoons dijon mustard
thyme sprigs, to garnish

Preheat the oven to 180°C (350°F/Gas 4). Wash the rabbits under cold water and pat dry with paper towels. Cut along both sides of each backbone with kitchen scissors and discard. Cut each rabbit into eight even-sized pieces, remove any fat and pat dry again.

Heat half the oil in a 2.5 litre (88 fl oz/10-cup) flameproof casserole dish. Brown the rabbit in batches, adding more oil when necessary, then remove from the dish.

Add the onion and bacon to the casserole dish and cook, stirring, for 5 minutes, or until lightly browned. Sprinkle the flour into the dish and mix. Stir with a wooden spoon to scrape the sediment from the base. Add the stock and wine, and stir until the sauce comes to the boil. Return the rabbit to the casserole dish and add the thyme leaves.

Cover and bake for about 1 hour 20 minutes, or until the rabbit is tender and the sauce has thickened. Stir in the combined cream and mustard. Garnish with thyme sprigs. Delicious with steamed vegetables.

Beef Pie

❧ SERVES 6
❧ PREPARATION TIME: 35 MINUTES
❧ COOKING TIME: 2 HOURS 45 MINUTES

FILLING

2 tablespoons olive oil

1 kg (2 lb 4 oz) trimmed chuck steak, cubed

1 large onion, chopped

1 large carrot, finely chopped

2 garlic cloves, crushed

2 tablespoons plain (all-purpose) flour

250 ml (9 fl oz/1 cup) beef stock

2 teaspoons thyme

1 tablespoon worcestershire sauce

PASTRY

250 g (9 oz/2 cups) plain (all-purpose) flour

150 g (5½ oz) chilled butter, cubed

1 egg yolk

2–3 tablespoons iced water

1 egg yolk, to glaze

1 tablespoon milk, to glaze

Lightly grease a 23 cm (9 inch) pie dish. To make the filling, heat half of the oil in a large frying pan and brown the meat in batches. Remove from the pan. Heat the remaining oil, add the onion, carrot and garlic and brown over medium heat. Return the meat to the pan and stir in the flour. Cook for 1 minute, then remove from the heat and slowly stir in the stock, mixing the flour in well. Add the thyme and worcestershire sauce and bring to the boil. Season to taste.

Reduce the heat to very low, cover and simmer for 1½–2 hours, or until the meat is tender. During the last 15 minutes of cooking, remove the lid and allow the liquid to reduce so that the sauce is very thick and suitable for filling a pie. Allow to cool completely.

To make the pastry, sift the flour into a large bowl. Using your fingertips, rub in the butter until it resembles fine breadcrumbs. Add the egg yolk and 2 tablespoons of the water and mix with a flat-bladed knife, using a cutting action, until the mixture comes together in beads. Add more water if the dough is too dry. Turn out onto a lightly floured work surface and gather together to form a smooth dough. Wrap in plastic wrap and refrigerate for 30 minutes.

Preheat the oven to 200°C (400°F/Gas 6). Divide the pastry in half and roll out one piece between two sheets of baking paper until large enough to line the pie dish. Line the dish with the pastry, fill with the cold filling and brush the pastry edges with water. Roll out the remaining pastry to cover the dish. Lay the pastry over the pie and gently press or pinch to seal the edges. Trim any excess pastry. Re-roll the scraps to make decorative shapes and press onto the pie.

Cut a few steam holes in the top of the pastry. Beat together the egg yolk and milk and brush over the top of the pie. Bake for 20–30 minutes, or until the pastry is golden and the filling is hot.

Classic Lasagne

❀ SERVES 8
❀ PREPARATION TIME: 40 MINUTES
❀ COOKING TIME: 1 HOUR 40 MINUTES

2 tablespoons olive oil
30 g (1 oz) butter
1 large onion, finely chopped
1 carrot, finely chopped
1 celery stalk, finely chopped
500 g (1 lb 2 oz) minced (ground) beef
150 g (5½ oz) chicken livers, finely
    chopped
250 ml (9 fl oz/1 cup) tomato passata
    (puréed tomatoes)
250 ml (9 fl oz/1 cup) red wine
2 tablespoons chopped flat-leaf
    (Italian) parsley
375 g (13 oz) fresh lasagne sheets
100 g (3½ oz/1 cup) freshly grated
    parmesan cheese

BÉCHAMEL SAUCE
60 g (2¼ oz) butter
40 g (1½ oz/⅓ cup) plain (all-purpose)
    flour
560 ml (19¼ fl oz/2¼ cups) milk
½ teaspoon freshly grated nutmeg

Heat the oil and butter in a heavy-based frying pan and cook the onion, carrot and celery over medium heat until softened, stirring constantly. Increase the heat, add the beef and brown well, breaking up any lumps with a fork. Add the chicken livers and cook until they change colour. Add the tomato passata, wine and parsley, and season to taste. Bring to the boil, reduce the heat and simmer for 45 minutes, then set aside.

To make the béchamel sauce, melt the butter in a saucepan over low heat. Add the flour and stir for 1 minute. Remove from the heat and gradually stir in the milk. Return to the heat and stir constantly until the sauce boils and begins to thicken. Simmer for another minute. Add the nutmeg and season to taste. Place a piece of plastic wrap on the surface of the sauce to prevent a skin forming, and set aside.

Cut the lasagne sheets to fit into a deep, rectangular ovenproof dish.

To assemble, preheat the oven to 180°C (350°F/Gas 4). Grease the ovenproof dish. Spread a thin layer of the meat sauce over the base and follow with a thin layer of béchamel. If the béchamel has cooled and become too thick, warm it gently to make spreading easier. Lay the lasagne sheets on top, gently pressing to push out any air. Continue the layers, finishing with the béchamel. Sprinkle with the parmesan and bake for 35–40 minutes, or until golden brown. Cool for 15 minutes before cutting.

NOTE: Instant lasagne can be used instead of fresh. Follow the manufacturer's instructions. If you prefer, you can leave out the chicken livers and increase the amount of mince.

Roast Beef with Yorkshire Puddings

❀ SERVES 6–8

❀ PREPARATION TIME: 15 MINUTES

❀ COOKING TIME: 1 HOUR 40 MINUTES

2 kg (4 lb 8 oz) piece roasting beef
  (such as scotch fillet, rump or sirloin)
2 garlic cloves, crushed
olive oil, for drizzling

YORKSHIRE PUDDINGS
90 g (3¼ oz/¾ cup) plain (all-purpose)
  flour
125 ml (4 fl oz/½ cup) milk
2 eggs

RED WINE GRAVY
2 tablespoons plain (all-purpose) flour
80 ml (2½ fl oz/⅓ cup) red wine
600 ml (21 fl oz) beef stock

Preheat the oven to 240°C (475°F/Gas 8). Rub beef with the garlic and some freshly cracked black pepper and drizzle with the oil. Bake on a rack in a baking dish for 20 minutes.

To make the Yorkshire puddings, sift the flour and ½ teaspoon salt into a large bowl, then make a well in the centre and whisk in the milk. In a separate bowl, whisk the eggs together until fluffy, then add to the batter and mix well. Add 125 ml (4 fl oz/½ cup) water and whisk until large bubbles form on the surface. Cover the bowl with plastic wrap and refrigerate for 1 hour.

Reduce the oven to 180°C (350°F/Gas 4) and continue to roast the meat for 1 hour for rare, or longer for well done. Cover loosely with foil and leave in a warm place while making the Yorkshire puddings.

Increase the oven to 220°C (425°F/Gas 7). Pour all the pan juices into a jug and spoon ½ teaspoon of the juices into twelve 80 ml (21½ fl oz/⅓ cup) patty or muffin tins. (Reserve the remaining juice for the gravy.) Heat the muffin tins in the oven until the fat is almost smoking. Whisk the batter until bubbles form on the surface. Pour into each muffin tin to three-quarters full. Bake for 20 minutes, or until puffed and lightly golden. Make the gravy while the Yorkshire puddings are baking.

To make the gravy, heat 2 tablespoons of the reserved pan juices in the baking dish on the stovetop over low heat. Add the flour and stir well, scraping the dish to incorporate all the sediment. Cook over medium heat for 1–2 minutes, stirring constantly, until the flour is well browned. Remove from the heat and gradually stir in the wine and stock. Return to the heat, stirring constantly, until the gravy boils and thickens. Simmer for 3 minutes. Season, to taste, with salt and freshly ground black pepper. Strain, if desired.

Serve the beef with the hot Yorkshire puddings and red wine gravy.

Baked Cannelloni Milanese

※ SERVES 4

※ PREPARATION TIME: 40 MINUTES

※ COOKING TIME: 1 HOUR 35 MINUTES

500 g (1 lb 2 oz) minced (ground) pork
    and veal
50 g (1¾ oz/½ cup) dry breadcrumbs
2 eggs, beaten
1 teaspoon dried oregano
100 g (3½ oz/1 cup) freshly grated
    parmesan cheese
12–15 instant cannelloni tubes
375 g (13 oz) fresh ricotta cheese
60 g (2¼ oz/½ cup) freshly grated
    cheddar cheese

TOMATO SAUCE
425 ml (15 fl oz) tinned tomato passata
    (puréed tomatoes)
425 g (15 oz) crushed tomatoes
2 garlic cloves, crushed
3 tablespoons chopped basil

Preheat the oven to 180°C (350°F/Gas 4). Lightly grease a deep rectangular casserole dish.

In a bowl, combine the pork and veal mince, breadcrumbs, egg, oregano and half the parmesan, and season to taste. Use a teaspoon to stuff the cannelloni tubes with the mixture. Set aside.

To make the tomato sauce, bring the tomato passata, tomato and garlic to the boil in a saucepan. Reduce the heat and simmer for 15 minutes. Add the basil and pepper, to taste, and stir well.

Spoon half the tomato sauce over the base of the prepared dish. Arrange the stuffed cannelloni tubes on top. Cover with the remaining sauce. Spread with ricotta cheese. Sprinkle with the combined remaining parmesan and cheddar cheese. Bake, covered with foil, for 1 hour. Uncover and bake for another 15 minutes, or until golden. Cut into squares to serve.

Beef Provençale

❀ SERVES 6
❀ PREPARATION TIME: 20 MINUTES
❀ COOKING TIME: 2 HOURS 25 MINUTES

1.5 kg (3 lb 5 oz) chuck steak, cut into
    3 cm (1¼ inch) cubes
2 tablespoons olive oil
1 small onion, sliced
375 ml (13 fl oz/1½ cups) red wine
2 tablespoons chopped flat-leaf (Italian)
    parsley
1 tablespoon chopped rosemary
1 tablespoon chopped thyme
2 bay leaves
250 g (9 oz) speck, rind removed, cut into
    1 x 2 cm (½ x ¾ inch) pieces
400 g (14 oz) tinned crushed tomatoes
250 ml (9 fl oz/1 cup) beef stock
500 g (1 lb 2 oz) baby carrots
45 g (1¾ oz/⅓ cup) pitted niçoise olives

In a bowl, combine the cubed beef with 1 tablespoon of the oil, the onion, 250 ml (9 fl oz/1 cup) of the wine and half the herbs. Cover with plastic wrap and marinate in the refrigerator overnight. Drain the beef, reserving the marinade. Heat the remaining oil in a large heavy-based saucepan and brown the beef and onion in batches. Remove from the pan.

Add the speck to the pan and cook for 3–5 minutes, or until crisp. Return the beef to the pan with the remaining wine and marinade and cook, scraping the residue from the base of the pan for 2 minutes, or until the wine has slightly reduced. Add the tomato and stock and bring to the boil. Reduce the heat, add the remaining herbs and season well. Cover and simmer for 1 hour 30 minutes. Add the carrots and olives and cook, uncovered, for another 30 minutes, or until the meat and the carrots are tender. Before serving, check the seasoning and adjust if necessary.

Veal Foyot

❀ SERVES 6
❀ PREPARATION TIME: 25 MINUTES
❀ COOKING TIME: 1 HOUR 35 MINUTES

50 g (1¾ oz) butter
1 onion, chopped
185 ml (6 fl oz/¾ cup) white wine
185 ml (6 fl oz/¾ cup) beef stock
1.5 kg (3 lb 5 oz) nut (cushion) of veal
80 g (2¾ oz/1 cup) fresh breadcrumbs
125 g (4½ oz) gruyère cheese, grated

Preheat the oven to 180°C (350°F/Gas 4). Melt half the butter in a saucepan and fry the onion until soft. Add the wine and stock, bring to the boil and boil for 2 minutes. Add ¼ teaspoon each of salt and white pepper. Remove from the heat and allow to cool.

Place the veal in a baking dish and rub with salt and white pepper. Pour the onion and wine mixture into the baking dish with the veal. Mix the breadcrumbs and cheese, and press firmly onto the veal to form a thick coating. Melt the remaining butter and pour over the cheese crust.

Roast the veal for about 1 hour 20 minutes. If the crust is browning too quickly, cover lightly with foil. Leave for 10 minutes before carving into 1 cm (½ inch) slices. Spoon pan juices over the top.

Beef Provençale

vegetables

Lemon and Herb Risotto with Fried Mushrooms

※ SERVES 4–6
※ PREPARATION TIME: 30 MINUTES
※ COOKING TIME: 50 MINUTES

1 litre (35 fl oz/4 cups) chicken or
    vegetable stock
pinch saffron threads
2 tablespoons olive oil
2 leeks, thinly sliced
2 garlic cloves, crushed
440 g (15½ oz/2 cups) risotto rice
2–3 teaspoons finely grated lemon zest
2 tablespoons lemon juice
2 tablespoons chopped flat-leaf (Italian)
    parsley
2 tablespoons snipped chives
2 tablespoons chopped oregano
75 g (2¾ oz/¾ cup) freshly grated
    parmesan cheese
100 g (3½ oz) mascarpone cheese

FRIED MUSHROOMS
30 g (1 oz) butter
1 tablespoon olive oil
200 g (7 oz) small flat mushrooms, cut
    into thick slices
1 tablespoon balsamic vinegar

Pour the stock into a saucepan and add the saffron threads. Bring to the boil, then reduce the heat, cover and keep at a low simmer.

Heat the olive oil in a large saucepan over medium heat. Add the leek, cook for 5 minutes, then add the garlic and cook for a further 5 minutes, or until golden. Add the rice and stir until well coated. Add half the lemon zest and half the juice, then add 125 ml (4 fl oz/½ cup) of the hot stock. Stir constantly over medium heat until all the liquid has been absorbed. Continue adding more liquid, 125 ml (4 fl oz/½ cup) at a time until all the liquid is absorbed and the rice is tender and creamy. (You may not need to use all the stock, or you may need a little extra — every risotto will be slightly different.)

Remove the pan from the heat. Stir in the herbs, parmesan, mascarpone and the remaining lemon zest and lemon juice. Cover and keep warm.

To cook the mushrooms, melt the butter with the olive oil in a large frying pan, add the sliced mushrooms and vinegar and cook, stirring, over high heat for about 6 minutes, or until the mushrooms are tender and all the liquid has been absorbed. Serve the risotto in large bowls topped with the fried mushrooms.

Borlotti Bean Moussaka

❈ SERVES 6
❈ PREPARATION TIME: 45 MINUTES
❈ COOKING TIME: 2 HOURS 30 MINUTES

250 g (9 oz/1¼ cups) dried borlotti
    (cranberry) beans
2 large eggplants (aubergines)
80 ml (2½ fl oz/⅓ cup) olive oil
1 garlic clove, crushed
1 onion, chopped
125 g (4½ oz) button mushrooms, sliced
2 x 440 g (15½ oz) tins peeled tomatoes,
    chopped
250 ml (9 fl oz/1 cup) red wine
1 tablespoon tomato paste (concentrated
    purée)
1 tablespoon chopped oregano

TOPPING
250 g (9 oz/1 cup) plain yoghurt
4 eggs, lightly beaten
500 ml (17 fl oz/2 cups) milk
¼ teaspoon paprika
50 g (1¾ oz/½ cup) freshly grated
    parmesan cheese
40 g (1½ oz/½ cup) fresh breadcrumbs

Soak the borlotti beans in cold water overnight. Rinse and drain well.

Put the borlotti beans in a large heavy-based saucepan, cover with water and bring to the boil. Reduce the heat and simmer for 1½ hours, or until tender. Drain the beans.

Meanwhile, slice the eggplant, sprinkle with salt and set aside for 30 minutes. Rinse and pat dry. Brush the eggplant slices with a little of the oil and cook under a preheated grill (broiler) for 3 minutes each side, or until golden. Drain on paper towel.

Preheat the oven to 200°C (400°F/Gas 6). Heat the remaining oil in a large heavy-based saucepan. Add the garlic and onion and cook over medium heat for 3 minutes, or until the onion is golden. Add the mushrooms and cook for 3 minutes, or until browned. Stir in the tomatoes, wine, tomato paste and oregano. Bring to the boil, reduce the heat and simmer for 40 minutes, or until the sauce has thickened.

To assemble the moussaka, spoon the borlotti beans into a large, ovenproof dish and top with the tomato sauce and eggplant slices.

To make the topping, whisk together the yoghurt, eggs, milk and paprika. Pour over the eggplant and set aside for 10 minutes. Combine the parmesan cheese and breadcrumbs and sprinkle over the moussaka. Bake for 45–60 minutes, or until the moussaka is heated through and the top is golden.

Tofu, Peanut and Noodle Stir-Fry

❀ SERVES 4
❀ PREPARATION TIME: 15 MINUTES
❀ COOKING TIME: 5 MINUTES

1 red capsicum (pepper)
250 g (9 oz) firm tofu
2 garlic cloves, crushed
1 teaspoon grated fresh ginger
80 ml (2½ fl oz/⅓ cup) kecap manis
90 g (3¼ oz/⅓ cup) peanut butter
2 tablespoons peanut or vegetable oil
500 g (1 lb 2 oz) hokkien (egg) noodles
1 onion, chopped
125 g (4½ oz) broccoli, cut into small
  florets

Cut the capsicum in half, remove the seeds and membrane and chop. Cut the tofu into 1.5 cm (⁵⁄₈ inch) cubes. Combine the tofu with the garlic, ginger and half the kecap manis in a small bowl. Put the peanut butter, 125 ml (4 fl oz/½ cup) water and remaining kecap manis in another bowl and mix.

Heat a wok over high heat, add the oil and swirl to coat the base and side. Drain the tofu and reserve the marinade. Cook the tofu in two batches in the hot oil until well browned. Remove from the wok.

Put the noodles in a large heatproof bowl. Cover with boiling water and leave for 1 minute. Drain and gently separate the noodles. Add the vegetables to the wok (add a little more oil if necessary) and stir-fry until just tender. Add the tofu, reserved marinade and noodles to the wok. Add the peanut butter mixture and toss until heated through.

Linguine with Roasted Vegetable Sauce

❀ SERVES 4
❀ PREPARATION TIME: 30 MINUTES
❀ COOKING TIME: 50 MINUTES

4 large red capsicums (peppers)
500 g (1 lb 2 oz) firm ripe tomatoes
3 large red onions
1 garlic bulb
125 ml (4 fl oz/½ cup) balsamic vinegar
60 ml (2 fl oz/¼ cup) olive oil
2 teaspoons sea salt
2 teaspoons freshly ground black pepper
500 g (1 lb 2 oz) linguine
100 g (3½ oz) parmesan cheese, shaved
100 g (3½ oz) black olives

Preheat the oven to 180°C (350°F/Gas 4). Cut the capsicums in half and remove the seeds and membrane. Cut the tomatoes and onions in half and separate and peel the garlic cloves. Arrange the vegetables in a large ovenproof dish in a single layer. Pour the vinegar and oil over them and sprinkle with the sea salt and pepper. Bake for 50 minutes. Allow to cool for 5 minutes before puréeing in a food processor for 3 minutes, or until the mixture is smooth. Season with more salt and pepper, if necessary.

When the vegetables are almost cooked, cook the linguine in a large saucepan of rapidly boiling salted water until *al dente*. Drain. Serve the roasted vegetable sauce over the linguine with the parmesan cheese, olives and some extra black pepper.

Tofu, Peanut and Noodle Stir-Fry

Spicy Chickpea and Vegetable Casserole

* SERVES 4
* PREPARATION TIME: 25 MINUTES
* COOKING TIME: 1 HOUR 30 MINUTES

330 g (11¾ oz/1½ cups) dried chickpeas
  (see Note)
2 tablespoons olive oil
1 large onion, chopped
1 garlic clove, crushed
3 teaspoons ground cumin
½ teaspoon chilli powder
½ teaspoon ground allspice
425 g (15 oz) tinned peeled tomatoes,
  crushed
375 ml (13 fl oz/1½ cups) vegetable stock
300 g (10½ oz) pumpkin (winter squash),
  cut into large cubes
150 g (5½ oz) green beans, topped and
  tailed
200 g (7 oz) baby (pattypan) squash, cut
  into quarters
2 tablespoons tomato paste (concentrated
  purée)
1 teaspoon dried oregano

Put the chickpeas in a large bowl. Cover with cold water and soak overnight. Drain.

Heat the oil in a large saucepan. Add the onion and garlic and stir-fry for 2 minutes, or until tender. Add the cumin, chilli powder and allspice. Stir-fry for 1 minute. Add the chickpeas, tomatoes and vegetable stock to the pan. Bring to the boil, then reduce the heat and simmer, covered, for 1 hour, stirring occasionally.

Add the pumpkin, beans, squash, tomato paste and oregano. Stir to combine. Simmer, covered, for another 15 minutes. Remove the lid from the pan and simmer, uncovered, for another 10 minutes to reduce and slightly thicken the sauce.

NOTE: A quick way to soak chickpeas is to place them in a large saucepan and cover with cold water. Bring to the boil, then remove from the heat and soak for 2 hours. If you are in a hurry, substitute tinned chickpeas. Drain and rinse thoroughly before use.

Vegetable Lasagne

※ SERVES 6
※ PREPARATION TIME: 40 MINUTES
※ COOKING TIME: 1 HOUR 15 MINUTES

3 large red capsicums (peppers)
2 large eggplants (aubergines)
2 tablespoons olive oil
1 large onion, chopped
3 garlic cloves, crushed
1 teaspoon dried mixed herbs
1 teaspoon dried oregano
500 g (1 lb 2 oz) mushrooms, sliced
440 g (15½ oz) tinned crushed tomatoes
440 g (15½ oz) tinned red kidney beans,
    drained
1 tablespoon sweet chilli sauce
250 g (9 oz) packet instant lasagne
500 g (1 lb 2 oz) English spinach, chopped
30 g (1 oz) basil leaves
90 g (3¼ oz) sun-dried tomatoes, sliced
25 g (1 oz/¼ cup) grated parmesan
    cheese
30 g (1 oz/¼ cup) grated cheddar cheese

CHEESE SAUCE
60 g (2¼ oz) butter
30 g (1 oz/¼ cup) plain (all-purpose)
    flour
500 ml (17 fl oz/2 cups) milk
600 g (1 lb 5 oz) ricotta cheese

Preheat the oven to 180°C (350°F/Gas 4). Brush a 28 x 35 cm (11¼ x 14 inch) ovenproof dish with oil.

Cut the capsicums in half, remove the seeds and membrane and cut into large flattish pieces. Cook, skin side up, under a hot grill (broiler) for 8 minutes, or until the skin is black and blistered. Cover with a damp tea towel (dish towel) and when cool, peel away the skin and cut the flesh into long thin strips. Set aside.

Slice the eggplant into 1 cm (½ inch) rounds and put in a large saucepan of boiling water. Cook for 1 minute, or until just tender. Drain, pat dry with paper towel and set aside.

Heat the oil in a large heavy-based frying pan and add the onion, garlic and herbs. Cook over medium heat for 5 minutes, or until the onion is soft. Add the mushrooms and cook for 1 minute. Add the crushed tomatoes, red kidney beans, chilli sauce and season to taste. Bring to the boil, reduce the heat and simmer for 15 minutes, or until the sauce thickens. Remove from the heat and set aside.

To make the cheese sauce, heat the butter in a saucepan and stir in the flour over medium heat for 1 minute, or until smooth. Remove from the heat and gradually stir in the milk. Return to the heat and stir constantly until the sauce boils and begins to thicken. Simmer for another minute. Add the ricotta and stir until smooth.

Dip the lasagne sheets, if necessary, in hot water to soften slightly and arrange four sheets on the base of the dish. Build up layers on top of the pasta, using half of the eggplant, spinach, basil, grilled capsicum strips, mushroom sauce and then the sun-dried tomatoes. Top with a layer of pasta and press gently. Repeat the layers, finishing with a layer of lasagne. Top with cheese sauce and sprinkle with the combined parmesan and cheddar cheeses. Bake for 45 minutes, or until the pasta is soft.

Pea, Egg and Ricotta Curry

❧ SERVES 4

❧ PREPARATION TIME: 15 MINUTES

❧ COOKING TIME: 30 MINUTES

4 hard-boiled eggs
1/2 teaspoon ground turmeric
2 small onions, finely chopped
45 ml (1 1/2 fl oz) ghee or vegetable oil
1 bay leaf
125 g (4 1/2 oz) baked ricotta cheese
    (see Note)
1 teaspoon finely chopped garlic
1 1/2 teaspoons ground coriander
1 1/2 teaspoons garam masala
1/2 teaspoon chilli powder (optional)
125 g (4 1/2 oz/ 1/2 cup) tinned peeled,
    chopped tomatoes
1 tablespoon tomato paste (concentrated
    purée)
1 tablespoon plain yoghurt
80 g (2 3/4 oz/ 1/2 cup) frozen peas
2 tablespoons finely chopped coriander
    (cilantro) leaves

Peel the eggs and coat them with the turmeric. Cut the ricotta into 1 cm (1/2 inch) cubes.

Melt the ghee in a large saucepan and cook the eggs over moderate heat for 2 minutes until they are light brown, stirring constantly. Set aside.

Add the bay leaf, onion and garlic to the pan and cook over moderately high heat, stirring frequently, until the mixture is well reduced and pale gold. Lower the heat if the mixture is browning too quickly. Add the ground coriander, garam masala and chilli powder, if using, and cook until fragrant.

Add the tomato, tomato paste and 125 ml (4 fl oz/ 1/2 cup) water. Cover and simmer for 5 minutes. Return the eggs to the pan with the ricotta, yoghurt, peas and 1/4 teaspoon salt and cook for 5 minutes. Remove the bay leaf, sprinkle with the coriander and serve immediately.

NOTE: Baked ricotta cheese is available from delicatessens and some supermarkets, but it is easy enough to prepare your own. Preheat the oven to 160°C (315°F/Gas 2–3). Slice the required amount of fresh ricotta (not cottage cheese or blended ricotta) into 3 cm (1 1/4 inch) thick slices. Place the ricotta on a lightly greased baking tray and bake for 25 minutes.

Spanokopita

❧ SERVES 4–6

❧ PREPARATION TIME: 25 MINUTES

❧ COOKING TIME: 1 HOUR

1.5 kg (3 lb 5 oz) silverbeet (Swiss chard)
60 ml (2 fl oz/¼ cup) olive oil
1 white onion, finely chopped
10 spring onions (scallions), finely
    chopped
1½ tablespoons chopped dill
200 g (7 oz) Greek feta cheese, crumbled
125 g (4½ oz/½ cup) cottage cheese
35 g (1¼ oz/⅓ cup) finely grated
    kefalotyri cheese (see Note)
¼ teaspoon freshly grated nutmeg
4 eggs, lightly beaten
10 sheets filo pastry
80 g (2¾ oz) butter, melted, to brush

Rinse and drain the silverbeet thoroughly. Discard the stems and shred the leaves. Finely chop the onion.

Heat the olive oil in a large frying pan, add the onion and cook, stirring, over medium heat for 5 minutes, or until softened. Add the spring onion and silverbeet and cook, covered, over medium heat for 5 minutes. Add the dill and cook, uncovered, for 3–4 minutes, or until most of the liquid has evaporated. Remove from the heat and cool to room temperature.

Preheat the oven to 180°C (350°F/Gas 4) and lightly grease a 20 x 25 cm (8 x 10 inch) 2.5 litre (88 fl oz/10-cup) ovenproof dish. Put the feta, cottage cheese and kefalotyri in a large bowl. Stir in the silverbeet mixture and add the nutmeg. Gradually add the eggs and combine well. Season to taste.

Line the base and sides of the dish with a sheet of filo pastry – keep the rest covered with a damp tea towel (dish towel) to prevent them from drying out. Brush with some of the melted butter and cover with another sheet of pastry. Butter the sheet and repeat in this way, using five sheets of pastry. Spoon the filling into the dish and level the surface. Fold the exposed pastry up and over to cover the top of the filling. Cover with a sheet of pastry, brush with the butter and continue until all the remaining sheets are used. Roughly trim the pastry with kitchen scissors then tuck the excess inside the wall of the dish.

Brush the top with the butter. Using a sharp knife, score the surface into squares. Sprinkle a few drops of cold water on top to prevent the pastry from curling. Bake for 45 minutes, or until puffed and golden. Rest at room temperature for 10 minutes before serving.

NOTE: Kefalotyri is a Greek cheese made from 100% pasteurised sheep's milk. It is a hard pale golden-yellow cheese with a tangy flavour and a sharp aroma. It is usually grated, like parmesan or pecorino. You can use pecorino if kefalotyri is unavailable.

Lentil Bhuja Casserole

🌿 SERVES 4–6
🌿 PREPARATION TIME: 40 MINUTES
🌿 COOKING TIME: 1 HOUR 10 MINUTES

400 g (13 oz/2 cups) green lentils
1 large onion
1 large potato
1 teaspoon ground cumin
1 teaspoon ground coriander
1 teaspoon ground turmeric
90 g (3¼ oz/¾ cup) plain (all-purpose)
    flour
vegetable oil, for pan-frying
2 tablespoons vegetable oil, extra
2 garlic cloves, crushed
1 tablespoon grated fresh ginger
250 ml (9 fl oz/1 cup) tomato passata
    (puréed tomatoes)
500 ml (17 fl oz/2 cups) vegetable stock
250 ml (9 fl oz/1 cup) cream
200 g (7 oz) green beans, topped and
    tailed
2 carrots, sliced
pitta bread, to serve

Cover the lentils with cold water and soak overnight. Drain well.

Grate the onion and potato and drain the excess liquid. Combine the lentils, onion, potato, cumin, coriander, turmeric and flour in a bowl, and mix well. Roll the mixture into walnut-sized balls and place them on a foil-lined tray. Cover and refrigerate for 30 minutes.

Heat the oil, about 2 cm (¾ inch) deep, in a frying pan. Add the lentil balls in small batches and fry over high heat for 5 minutes, or until golden brown. Drain on paper towel.

Heat the extra oil in a large saucepan. Add the garlic and ginger and cook, stirring, over medium heat for 1 minute. Stir in the tomato passata, vegetable stock and cream. Bring to the boil, reduce the heat and simmer, uncovered, for 10 minutes. Add the lentil balls, beans and carrot, cover and simmer for 35 minutes, stirring occasionally. Serve with pitta bread.

NOTE: Make sure your hands are dry when shaping the lentil mixture into balls. The lentil balls can be made a day ahead and stored in an airtight container in the refrigerator.

Filo Risotto Pie

❀ SERVES 8
❀ PREPARATION TIME: 45 MINUTES
❀ COOKING TIME: 1 HOUR 45 MINUTES

2 large red capsicums (peppers)

RISOTTO
250 ml (9 fl oz/1 cup) white wine
1 litre (35 fl oz/4 cups) vegetable stock
2 tablespoons olive oil
1 garlic clove, crushed
1 leek, white part only, sliced
1 fennel bulb, thinly sliced
440 g (15½ oz/2 cups) arborio rice
60 g (2¼ oz) freshly grated parmesan
    cheese

10 sheets filo pastry
60 ml (2 fl oz/¼ cup) olive oil
500 g (1 lb 2 oz) English spinach,
    blanched
250 g (9 oz) feta cheese, sliced
1 tablespoon sesame seeds

Cut the capsicums in half. Remove the seeds and membrane and then cut into large, flattish pieces. Grill (broil) until the skin blackens and blisters. Place on a cutting board, cover with a tea towel (dish towel) and allow to cool. Peel the capsicum and cut the flesh into smaller pieces.

To make the risotto, put the wine and stock into a large saucepan. Bring to the boil and reduce the heat.

Heat the oil and garlic in a large heavy-based saucepan. Add the leek and fennel, cook over medium heat for 5 minutes, or until lightly browned. Add the rice and stir for 3 minutes, or until the rice is translucent. Add 250 ml (9 fl oz/1 cup) of the stock mixture to the rice and stir constantly until the liquid is absorbed. Continue adding liquid, 125 ml (4 fl oz/½ cup) at a time, stirring constantly until all the stock mixture has been used and the rice is tender. (This will take about 40 minutes.) Make sure the liquid stays hot as the risotto will become gluggy if it isn't. Remove from the heat, stir in the parmesan and season. Set aside to cool slightly.

Brush each sheet of filo with olive oil and fold in half lengthways. Arrange like overlapping spokes on a wheel, in a 23 cm (9 inch) spring-form cake tin, with one side of the pastry hanging over the side of the tin.

Preheat the oven to 180°C (350°F/Gas 4). Spoon half the risotto mixture over the pastry and top with half the red capsicum, half the spinach and half the feta. Repeat with the remaining risotto, capsicum, spinach and feta.

Fold the pastry over the filling, brush lightly with oil and sprinkle with sesame seeds. Bake for 50 minutes, or until the pastry is crisp and golden and the pie is heated through.

Vegetable Donburi

※ SERVES 4
※ PREPARATION TIME: 20 MINUTES
※ COOKING TIME: 35 MINUTES

100 g (3½ oz) green beans
2 slender eggplants (aubergines)
5 spring onions (scallions)
440 g (15½ oz/2 cups) Japanese short-grain rice
10 g (¼ oz) dried whole shiitake mushrooms
2 tablespoons vegetable oil
1 onion, sliced
100 ml (3½ fl oz) shoyu (Japanese soy sauce) (see Note)
100 ml (3½ fl oz) mirin
55 g (2 oz/¼ cup) sugar
4 eggs, lightly beaten

Trim the green beans and cut them into 4 cm (1½ inch) lengths. Slice the eggplants diagonally and cut the spring onions into 2 cm (¾ inch) lengths.

Wash the rice and put in a saucepan with 625 ml (21½ fl oz/2½ cups) water. Bring to the boil then reduce the heat and simmer, covered, for 15 minutes. Leave, covered, for 10 minutes.

Soak the mushrooms in 420 ml (14½ fl oz/1⅔ cups) boiling water for 15 minutes. Drain and reserve the soaking liquid. Remove the stems. Cut the caps in half.

Heat the oil in a deep frying pan. Cook the onion over medium heat for 4 minutes, or until softened but not browned. Add the eggplant and cook for 3–4 minutes, or until softened. Add the beans, mushrooms and spring onion and cook for about 3 minutes, or until almost cooked. Combine the shoyu, mushroom soaking liquid, mirin and sugar, and stir through the vegetables. Simmer for 4 minutes.

Pour the egg over the vegetables, cover and simmer for 1 minute, or until partly cooked. Serve the rice in bowls, spoon on the vegetable mixture and pour on the cooking sauce.

NOTE: Shoyu (Japanese soy sauce) is available from Asian speciality food stores.

Giant Conchiglie with Ricotta and Rocket

❀ SERVES 6
❀ PREPARATION TIME: 50 MINUTES
❀ COOKING TIME: 1 HOUR

40 giant conchiglie (shell pasta)

FILLING
500 g (1 lb 2 oz) ricotta cheese
100 g (3½ oz/1 cup) grated parmesan
    cheese
150 g (5½ oz) rocket (arugula), finely
    shredded
1 egg, lightly beaten
185 g (6½ oz) marinated globe artichokes,
    finely chopped
80 g (2¾ oz) sun-dried (sun-blushed)
    tomatoes, finely chopped
95 g (3¼ oz) sun-dried (sun-blushed)
    capsicum (pepper), finely chopped

CHEESE SAUCE
60 g (2¼ oz) butter
30 g (1 oz/¼ cup) plain (all-purpose)
    flour
750 ml (26 fl oz/3 cups) milk
100 g (3½ oz) gruyère cheese, grated
2 tablespoons chopped basil

600 ml (21 fl oz) bottled pasta sauce
2 tablespoons oregano, chopped
2 tablespoons basil

Cook the giant conchiglie in a large saucepan of rapidly boiling salted water until *al dente*. Drain and arrange the shells on two non-stick baking trays to prevent them sticking together. Cover lightly with plastic wrap.

To make the filling, combine all the ingredients in a large bowl. Spoon the filling into the shells, taking care not to overfill them or they will split.

To make the cheese sauce, melt the butter in a small saucepan over low heat. Add the flour and stir for 1 minute, or until golden and smooth. Remove from the heat and gradually stir in the milk. Return to the heat and stir constantly until the sauce boils and begins to thicken. Simmer for a further minute. Remove from the heat and stir in the gruyère cheese with the basil and season to taste.

Preheat the oven to 180°C (350°F/Gas 4). Spread 250 ml (9 fl oz/1 cup) of the cheese sauce over the base of a 3 litre (104 fl oz/12-cup) capacity ovenproof dish. Arrange the filled conchiglie over the sauce, top with the remaining sauce and bake for 30 minutes, or until the sauce is golden.

Pour the bottled pasta sauce in a saucepan and add the oregano. Cook over medium heat for 5 minutes, or until heated through. To serve, divide the sauce among the warmed serving plates, top with the conchiglie and sprinkle with the basil leaves.

Vegetarian Phad Thai

❀ SERVES 4
❀ PREPARATION TIME: 20 MINUTES
❀ COOKING TIME: 5 MINUTES

400 g (14 oz) flat rice stick noodles
1 small red capsicum (pepper)
100 g (3½ oz) fried tofu puffs
60 ml (2 fl oz/¼ cup) soy sauce
2 tablespoons lime juice
1 tablespoon soft brown sugar
2 teaspoons sambal oelek (see Note)
2 tablespoons peanut oil
2 eggs, lightly beaten
1 onion, cut into thin wedges
2 garlic cloves, crushed
6 spring onions (scallions), thinly sliced on
   the diagonal
25 g (1 oz) chopped coriander (cilantro)
   leaves
90 g (3¼ oz/1 cup) bean sprouts,
   trimmed
40 g (1½ oz/¼ cup) chopped roasted
   peanuts

Soak the noodles in warm water for 15–20 minutes, or until tender. Drain, then set aside.

Cut the capsicum in half, remove the seeds and membrane and cut into thin strips. Cut the fried tofu puffs into 5 mm (¼ inch) wide strips.

To make the stir-fry sauce, combine the soy sauce, lime juice, brown sugar and sambal oelek in a small bowl.

Heat a wok over high heat. Add enough oil to coat the base and side. Add the egg and swirl to form a thin omelette. Cook for 30 seconds, or until just set. Remove from the wok, roll up, then thinly slice.

Heat the remaining oil in the wok. Add the onion, garlic and capsicum and cook over high heat for 2–3 minutes, or until the onion softens. Add the noodles, tossing well. Stir in the slices of omelette, the spring onion, tofu and half of the coriander. Pour in the stir-fry sauce, then toss to coat the noodles. Sprinkle with the bean sprouts and top with roasted peanuts and the remaining coriander. Serve immediately.

NOTE: Sambal oelek is a Southeast Asian chilli paste.

Cheese~Filled Crepes with Tomato Sauce

❧ MAKES ABOUT 12
❧ PREPARATION TIME: 25 MINUTES
❧ COOKING TIME: 1 HOUR 10 MINUTES

CREPES

165 g (5¾ oz/1⅓ cups) plain
   (all-purpose) flour
500 ml (17 fl oz/2 cups) milk
3 eggs, lightly beaten
30 g (1 oz) butter, melted

TOMATO SAUCE

2 tablespoons olive oil
1 garlic clove, crushed
400 g (14 oz) tinned crushed tomatoes
3 tablespoons chopped flat-leaf (Italian)
   parsley

CHEESE FILLING

400 g (14 oz) ricotta cheese, crumbled
100 g (3½ oz/⅔ cup) grated mozzarella
   cheese
25 g (1 oz/¼ cup) freshly grated
   parmesan cheese
pinch freshly grated nutmeg
3 tablespoons chopped flat-leaf (Italian)
   parsley

25 g (1 oz/¼ cup) freshly grated
   parmesan cheese
2 tablespoons extra virgin olive oil,
   to drizzle

To make the crepes, sift the flour and ½ teaspoon salt into a bowl. Make a well in the centre and gradually add the milk, stirring constantly until the mixture is smooth. Add the eggs, little by little, beating well until smooth. Cover and set aside for 30 minutes.

Meanwhile, to make the tomato sauce, heat the oil in a heavy-based frying pan and add the garlic. Cook for 30 seconds over low heat until just golden, then add the tomatoes and 125 ml (4 fl oz/½ cup) water and season well. Simmer over low heat for 30 minutes, or until the sauce has reduced and thickened. Stir in the parsley.

Heat a crepe pan or non-stick frying pan and brush lightly with the melted butter. Pour 60 ml (2 fl oz/¼ cup) of batter into the pan, swirling quickly to thinly cover the base. Cook for 1 minute, or until the underside is golden. Turn and cook the other side until golden. Transfer to a plate and continue with the remaining batter, stacking the crepes as you go.

Preheat the oven to 200°C (400°F/Gas 6) and lightly grease a shallow ovenproof dish.

To make the filling, mix all the ingredients together and season well.

To assemble, spread 1 heaped tablespoon of filling over each crepe, leaving a 1 cm (½ inch) border. Fold the crepe in half and then in quarters. Place in the ovenproof dish, so that they overlap but are not crowded. Spoon the tomato sauce over the crepes, sprinkle with the parmesan and drizzle with the extra virgin olive oil. Bake for 20 minutes, or until heated through.

NOTE: The crepes can be made up to 3 days in advance but must be refrigerated with baking paper to separate them.

Oriental Mushrooms with Hokkien Noodles

✿ SERVES 4

✿ PREPARATION TIME: 35 MINUTES

✿ COOKING TIME: 10 MINUTES

250 g (9 oz) hokkien (egg) noodles
1 red capsicum (pepper)
1 teaspoon sesame oil
1 tablespoon peanut oil
2 garlic cloves, crushed
2 tablespoons grated fresh ginger
6 spring onions (scallions), sliced
200 g (7 oz) oyster mushrooms
200 g (7 oz) shiitake mushrooms, sliced
125 g (4½ oz) snipped garlic chives
40 g (1½ oz/¼ cup) cashew nuts
2 tablespoons kecap manis (see Note)
60 ml (2 fl oz/¼ cup) salt-reduced
    soy sauce

Soak the hokkien noodles in boiling water for
2 minutes. Drain and set them aside.

Cut the red capsicum in half, remove the seeds and
membrane and slice.

Heat the oils in a wok and swirl to coat the base and
side. Add the garlic, ginger and spring onion. Stir-fry
over high heat for 2 minutes. Add the red capsicum and
the oyster and shiitake mushrooms and stir-fry over
high heat for 3 minutes, or until the mushrooms are
golden brown.

Stir in the drained noodles. Add the chives, cashews,
kecap manis and soy sauce. Stir-fry for 3 minutes, or
until the noodles are coated in the sauce.

NOTE: Kecap manis is an Indonesian sweet soy sauce. If you
are unable to find it, use soy sauce sweetened with a little soft
brown sugar.

Vegetarian Noodles

* SERVES 4
* PREPARATION TIME: 25 MINUTES
* COOKING TIME: 15 MINUTES

15 g (½ oz) dried shiitake mushrooms
225 g (8 oz) tinned bamboo shoots
½ small red capsicum (pepper)
1 small green capsicum (pepper)
400 g (14 oz) fresh flat egg noodles
2–3 tablespoons peanut or sunflower oil
1 small carrot, cut into thin batons
150 g (5½ oz) baby corn, quartered
   lengthways
150 g (5½ oz) snow peas (mangetout), cut
   into thin batons
90 g (3¼ oz/1 cup) bean sprouts,
   trimmed
40 g (1½ oz) Chinese cabbage (wong
   bok), finely shredded
1 tablespoon thin strips fresh ginger
2 tablespoons vegetable oyster sauce
1 tablespoon mushroom soy sauce
1 tablespoon light soy sauce
1 tablespoon Chinese rice wine
1 teaspoon sesame oil
ground white pepper, to taste
coriander (cilantro) leaves, to garnish

Cover the mushrooms in boiling water and soak for 20 minutes. Drain. Discard the woody stalks and thinly slice the caps. Drain the bamboo shoots and cut into thin batons. Cut the capsicums in half, remove the seeds and membrane and cut into thin batons.

Cook the noodles in a large saucepan of boiling water for 1 minute, stirring to separate. Drain, rinse under cold running water and drain again.

Heat a wok over high heat, add 1 tablespoon of the oil and swirl to coat the base and side. Stir-fry the carrot and corn for 1–2 minutes, then add the bamboo shoots and stir-fry for a further 1–2 minutes, or until just cooked but still crisp. Remove the vegetables from the wok.

Reheat the wok (add 2 teaspoons peanut oil if necessary) and add the snow peas and red and green capsicum. Stir-fry for 1–2 minutes, or until just cooked but still crisp. Add to the carrot and corn mixture. Reheat the wok (add another 2 teaspoons peanut oil if needed), then add the bean sprouts, Chinese cabbage and mushrooms and stir-fry for 30 seconds, or until wilted. Add the ginger and stir-fry for a further 1–2 minutes. Remove from the wok and add to the other vegetables.

Heat the remaining oil in the wok, and quickly stir-fry the noodles for 1–2 minutes, or until heated through, taking care not to let them break up. Stir in the oyster sauce, mushroom soy sauce, light soy sauce and rice wine and stir thoroughly. Return all the vegetables to the wok and stir gently for 1–2 minutes, or until well combined with the noodles. Drizzle with the sesame oil, season with white pepper and garnish with the coriander leaves. Serve immediately.

Baked Eggplant with Tomato and Mozzarella

❧ SERVES 6

❧ PREPARATION TIME: 20 MINUTES

❧ COOKING TIME: 40 MINUTES

6 large slender eggplants (aubergines),
    halved lengthways, leaving the stems
    attached
100 ml (3½ fl oz) olive oil
2 onions, finely chopped
2 garlic cloves, crushed
400 g (14 oz) tinned chopped tomatoes
1 tablespoon tomato paste (concentrated
    purée)
3 tablespoons chopped flat-leaf (Italian)
    parsley
1 tablespoon chopped oregano
125 g (4½ oz) mozzarella cheese, grated

Preheat the oven to 180°C (350°F/Gas 4). Score the eggplant flesh by cutting a criss-cross pattern with a sharp knife. Heat 2 tablespoons of the oil in a large frying pan, add six eggplant halves and cook for 2–3 minutes each side, or until the flesh is soft. Remove. Add another 2 tablespoons of the oil and the remaining eggplant. Cool slightly and scoop out the flesh, leaving a 2 mm (¹⁄₁₆ inch) border. Chop the flesh and reserve the shells.

In the same pan, heat the remaining oil and cook the onion over medium heat for 5 minutes. Add the garlic and cook for 30 seconds, then add the tomato, tomato paste, herbs and eggplant flesh, and cook, stirring occasionally, over low heat for 8–10 minutes, or until the sauce is thick and pulpy. Season well.

Arrange the eggplant shells in a lightly greased baking dish and spoon in the tomato filling. Sprinkle with the mozzarella and bake for 5–10 minutes.

Chilli Satay Noodles

❧ SERVES 4–6

❧ PREPARATION TIME: 10 MINUTES

❧ COOKING TIME: 10 MINUTES

500 g (1 lb 2 oz) thin fresh egg noodles
1 tablespoon vegetable oil
1 teaspoon sesame oil
50 g (1¾ oz/⅓ cup) peanuts
2 small red chillies, sliced
4 slender eggplants (aubergines), sliced
200 g (7 oz) sugar snap peas, trimmed
100 g (3½ oz) bean sprouts, trimmed
60 g (2¼ oz/¼ cup) crunchy peanut butter
1 tablespoon hoisin sauce
80 ml (2½ fl oz/⅓ cup) coconut milk
2 tablespoons lime juice
1 tablespoon Thai sweet chilli sauce

Add the noodles to a large saucepan of boiling water and cook for 3 minutes. Drain, rinse well under cold running water and drain again. Heat the oils in a wok or frying pan. Add the peanuts and toss over high heat for 1 minute, or until golden. Add the chillies, eggplant and sugar snap peas and cook over high heat for 2 minutes. Reduce the heat to medium and add the noodles and the bean sprouts. Toss for 1 minute, or until combined.

Blend the peanut butter, hoisin sauce, coconut milk, lime juice and chilli sauce until almost smooth. Add to the noodles. Toss over medium heat until the noodles are coated and the sauce is heated through.

Baked Eggplant with Tomato and Mozzarella

Braised Vegetables with Cashews

❀ SERVES 4

❀ PREPARATION TIME: 15 MINUTES

❀ COOKING TIME: 10 MINUTES

1 tablespoon peanut oil

2 garlic cloves, crushed

2 teaspoons grated fresh ginger

300 g (10½ oz) choy sum, cut into 10 cm (4 inch) lengths

150 g (5½ oz) baby corn, sliced in half lengthways

185 ml (6 fl oz/¾ cup) chicken or vegetable stock

200 g (7 oz) sliced tinned bamboo shoots

150 g (5½ oz) oyster mushrooms, halved

2 teaspoons cornflour (cornstarch)

2 tablespoons oyster sauce

2 teaspoons sesame oil

90 g (3¼ oz/1 cup) bean sprouts, trimmed

steamed rice, to serve

70 g (2½ oz) unsalted cashew nuts, toasted, to serve

Heat a wok over medium heat, add the peanut oil and swirl to coat the base and side. Add the garlic and ginger and stir-fry for 1 minute. Increase the heat to high, add the choy sum and baby corn and stir-fry for another minute.

Add the stock and continue to cook for 3–4 minutes, or until the choy sum stems are just tender. Add the bamboo shoots and mushrooms and cook for 1 minute.

Combine the cornflour and 1 tablespoon water in a small bowl and mix into a paste. Stir the cornflour mixture and oyster sauce into the vegetables and cook for 1–2 minutes, or until the sauce is slightly thickened. Stir in the sesame oil and bean sprouts and serve immediately on a bed of steamed rice sprinkled with the toasted cashews.

Harvest Pie

PASTRY

125 g (4½ oz) butter, chopped
250 g (9 oz/2 cups) plain (all-purpose)
    flour
60 ml (2 fl oz/¼ cup) iced water

FILLING

1 tablespoon olive oil
1 onion, finely chopped
1 small red capsicum (pepper), seeded,
    membrane removed and chopped
1 small green capsicum (pepper), seeded,
    membrane removed and chopped
150 g (5½ oz) pumpkin (winter squash),
    chopped
1 small potato, chopped
100 g (3½ oz) broccoli, cut into small
    florets
1 carrot, chopped
50 g (1¾ oz) butter
30 g (1 oz/¼ cup) plain (all-purpose)
    flour, extra
250 ml (9 fl oz/1 cup) milk
2 egg yolks
60 g (2¼ oz/½ cup) grated cheddar
    cheese
1 egg, lightly beaten, to glaze

Preheat the oven to 180°C (350°F/Gas 4). To make the pastry, sift the flour into a large bowl. Using your fingertips, rub in the butter until the mixture resembles fine breadcrumbs. Add almost all the water and mix with a flat-bladed knife, using a cutting action until the mixture forms a firm dough, adding more water if necessary. Turn onto a lightly floured work surface and press together until smooth. Divide the dough in half, roll out one portion and line a deep 21 cm (8¼ inch) fluted flan (tart) tin. Refrigerate for 20 minutes. Roll the remaining pastry out to a 25 cm (10 inch) diameter circle. Cut into strips and lay half of them on a sheet of baking paper, leaving a 1 cm (½ inch) gap between each strip. Interweave the remaining strips to form a lattice pattern. Cover with plastic wrap and refrigerate, keeping flat, until firm.

Cut a sheet of baking paper to cover the pastry-lined tin. Spread a layer of baking beads or uncooked rice over the paper. Bake for 10 minutes, remove from the oven and discard the paper and beads. Bake for another 10 minutes, or until lightly golden. Allow to cool.

To make the filling, heat the oil in a frying pan. Add the onion and cook for 2 minutes, or until soft. Add the capsicum and cook, stirring, for 3 minutes. Steam or boil the remaining vegetables until just tender. Drain and cool. Mix the onion, capsicum and other vegetables in a large bowl. Heat the butter in a small saucepan. Add the flour and cook, stirring, for 2 minutes. Add the milk gradually, stirring over medium heat until the mixture boils and thickens. Boil for 1 minute and then remove from the heat. Add the egg yolks and cheese and stir until smooth.

Pour the sauce over the vegetables and stir to combine. Pour the mixture into the pastry case and brush the edges with the egg. Using the baking paper to lift, invert the pastry lattice over the vegetables. Remove the paper, trim the pastry edges and brush with the egg, sealing it to the cooked pastry. Brush the top with egg and bake for 30 minutes, or until golden brown.

Sweet Vegetable Curry

❀ SERVES 4
❀ PREPARATION TIME: 20 MINUTES
❀ COOKING TIME: 40 MINUTES

2 carrots
1 parsnip
1 potato
1 green capsicum (pepper)
2 tablespoons oil
2 onions, chopped
1 teaspoon ground cardamom
$\frac{1}{4}$ teaspoon ground cloves
1 $\frac{1}{2}$ teaspoons cumin seeds
1 teaspoon ground coriander
1 teaspoon ground turmeric
1 teaspoon brown mustard seeds
$\frac{1}{2}$ teaspoon chilli powder
2 teaspoons grated fresh ginger
330 ml (11$\frac{1}{4}$ fl oz/1$\frac{1}{3}$ cups) vegetable
    stock
185 ml (6 fl oz/$\frac{3}{4}$ cup) apricot nectar
2 tablespoons fruit chutney
200 g (7 oz) small button mushrooms
300 g (10$\frac{1}{2}$ oz) cauliflower, cut into small
    florets
25 g ($\frac{3}{4}$ oz/$\frac{1}{4}$ cup) ground almonds

Cut the carrots, parsnip and potato into 2 cm ($\frac{3}{4}$ inch) pieces. Cut the capsicum in half, remove the seeds and membrane and cut into 2 cm ($\frac{3}{4}$ inch) squares.

Heat the oil in a large heavy-based saucepan. Add the onion and cook over medium heat for 4 minutes, or until just soft. Add the cardamom, cloves, cumin seeds, ground coriander, turmeric, mustard seeds, chilli powder and ginger and cook, stirring, for 1 minute or until aromatic.

Add the carrot, parsnip, potato, vegetable stock, apricot nectar and fruit chutney to the pan. Cook, covered, over medium heat for 25 minutes, stirring occasionally.

Stir in the capsicum, mushrooms and cauliflower. Simmer for 10 minutes, or until the vegetables are tender. Stir in the ground almonds and serve with rice.

NOTE: Any vegetables can be used in this curry. For example, broccoli, zucchini (courgette), red capsicum (pepper) or orange sweet potato would be suitable.

Mushroom Nut Roast with Tomato Sauce

❋ SERVES 6
❋ PREPARATION TIME: 30 MINUTES
❋ COOKING TIME: 1 HOUR

2 tablespoons olive oil
1 large onion, diced
2 garlic cloves, crushed
300 g ($10^{1}/_{2}$ oz) cap mushrooms, finely
    chopped
200 g (7 oz) cashew nuts
200 g (7 oz) brazil nuts
125 g ($4^{1}/_{2}$ oz/1 cup) grated cheddar
    cheese
25 g (1 oz/$^{1}/_{4}$ cup) freshly grated
    parmesan cheese
1 egg, lightly beaten
2 tablespoons snipped chives
80 g ($2^{3}/_{4}$ oz/1 cup) fresh wholemeal
    (whole-wheat) breadcrumbs
chives, extra, to garnish

TOMATO SAUCE
$1^{1}/_{2}$ tablespoons olive oil
1 onion, finely chopped
1 garlic clove, crushed
400 g (14 oz) tinned chopped tomatoes
1 tablespoon tomato paste (concentrated
    purée)
1 teaspoon caster (superfine) sugar

Grease a 14 x 21 cm ($5^{1}/_{2}$ x $8^{1}/_{4}$ inch) loaf (bar) tin and line the base with baking paper.

Heat the oil in a frying pan and add the onion, garlic and mushrooms. Fry until soft, then cool.

Process the nuts in a food processor until finely chopped, but do not overprocess. Preheat the oven to 180°C (350°F/Gas 4).

Combine the cooled mushroom mixture, chopped nuts, cheddar, parmesan, egg, snipped chives and the breadcrumbs in a bowl. Mix well and season to taste. Press into the loaf tin and bake for 45 minutes, or until firm. Leave for 5 minutes, then turn out and garnish with the extra chives. Cut into slices to serve.

Meanwhile, to make the tomato sauce, heat the oil in a saucepan, add the onion and garlic and cook, stirring frequently, for 5 minutes, or until soft but not brown. Stir in the tomato, tomato paste, sugar and 80 ml ($2^{1}/_{2}$ fl oz/$^{1}/_{3}$ cup) water. Simmer gently for 3–5 minutes, or until slightly thickened. Season. Serve the tomato sauce with the sliced nut roast.

NOTE: For a variation, use a different mixture of nuts and add some seeds. You can use nuts such as pecans, almonds, hazelnuts (without skins) and pine nuts. Suitable seeds to use include sesame, pumpkin or sunflower seeds.

Potato Noodles with Vegetables

☙ SERVES 4
☙ PREPARATION TIME: 25 MINUTES
☙ COOKING TIME: 25 MINUTES

4 spring onions (scallions)
2 carrots
500 g (1 lb 2 oz) baby bok choy (pak
    choy) or 250 g (9 oz) spinach
300 g (10½ oz) dried potato starch
    noodles (see Notes)
10 g (¼ oz/⅓ cup) black fungus
    (see Notes)
60 ml (2 fl oz/¼ cup) sesame oil
2 tablespoons vegetable oil
3 garlic cloves, finely chopped
4 cm (1½ inch) piece fresh ginger, grated
60 ml (2 fl oz/¼ cup) Japanese soy sauce
    (see Notes)
2 tablespoons mirin
1 teaspoon sugar
2 tablespoons sesame and seaweed sprinkle
    (see Notes)

Finely chop two of the spring onions. Slice the remaining spring onions into 4 cm (1½ inch) pieces. Cut the carrots into 4 cm (1½ inch) batons. Roughly chop the baby bok choy.

Cook the noodles in a large saucepan of boiling water for about 5 minutes, or until they are translucent. Drain and rinse thoroughly under cold running water until the noodles are cold (this will also remove any excess starch). Use scissors to roughly chop the noodles into shorter lengths (this will make them easier to eat with chopsticks).

Pour hot water over the black fungus and soak for about 10 minutes.

Heat 1 tablespoon of the sesame oil with the vegetable oil in a large heavy-based frying pan or wok. Cook the garlic, ginger and finely chopped spring onion for 3 minutes over medium heat, stirring regularly. Add the carrot and stir-fry for 1 minute. Add the drained cooled noodles, sliced spring onion, bok choy, remaining sesame oil, the soy sauce, mirin and sugar. Toss well to coat the noodles with the sauce. Cover and cook over low heat for 2 minutes. Add the drained fungus, then cover and cook for 2 minutes. Scatter over the sesame and seaweed sprinkle and serve immediately.

NOTES : Potato starch noodles are also known as Korean pasta and are available from Asian food stores.
   Dried black fungus, Japanese soy sauce and sesame and seaweed sprinkle are all available from Asian food stores.

Minestrone Soup with Rice

☙ SERVES 6

☙ PREPARATION TIME: 20 MINUTES

☙ COOKING TIME: 2 HOURS 30 MINUTES

225 g (8 oz) dried borlotti (cranberry)
    beans
55 g (2 oz) butter
1 onion, finely chopped
1 garlic clove, finely chopped
3 tablespoons finely chopped flat-leaf
    (Italian) parsley
2 sage leaves
100 g (3½ oz) pancetta, cubed
2 celery stalks, halved, then sliced
2 carrots, sliced
3 potatoes, peeled
1 teaspoon tomato paste (concentrated
    purée)
400 g (14 oz) tinned chopped tomatoes
8 basil leaves
3 litres (105 fl oz/12 cups) chicken or
    vegetable stock
2 zucchini (courgettes), sliced
225 g (8 oz) fresh peas
125 g (4½ oz) green beans, cut into 4 cm
    (1½ inch) lengths
¼ cabbage, shredded
220 g (7¾ oz/1 cup) risotto rice
freshly grated parmesan cheese, to serve

Put the dried beans in a large bowl, cover with cold water and soak overnight. Drain and rinse under cold water.

Melt the butter in a saucepan and add the onion, garlic, parsley, sage and pancetta. Cook over low heat, stirring once or twice, for 10 minutes, or until the onion is softened but not browned. Add the celery, carrot and potatoes, and cook for 5 minutes. Stir in the tomato paste, tomato, basil and borlotti beans. Season with freshly ground black pepper. Pour in the stock and bring slowly to the boil. Cover and leave to simmer for 2 hours, stirring once or twice.

If the potatoes have not broken up by the end of the 2 hours, roughly break them with a fork against the side of the pan. Season to taste then add the zucchini, peas, green beans, cabbage and rice. Simmer for a further 15–20 minutes, or until the rice is cooked. Divide among six soup bowls and sprinkle with a little parmesan cheese, to serve.

Tortellini with Eggplant

❄ SERVES 4
❄ PREPARATION TIME: 10 MINUTES
❄ COOKING TIME: 20 MINUTES

1 red capsicum (pepper)
500 g (1 lb 2 oz) eggplant (aubergine)
500 g (1 lb 2 oz) fresh cheese and spinach
    tortellini
60 ml (2 fl oz/¼ cup) vegetable oil
2 garlic cloves, crushed
425 g (15 oz) tinned crushed tomatoes
250 ml (9 fl oz/1 cup) vegetable stock
25 g (1 oz) chopped basil

Cut the capsicum in half, remove the seeds and membrane and cut into small squares. Cut the eggplant into small cubes.

Cook the tortellini in a large saucepan of rapidly boiling salted water until *al dente*. Drain and return to the pan.

While the pasta is cooking, heat the oil in a large frying pan, add the garlic and red capsicum and stir over medium heat for 1 minute. Add the eggplant to the pan and stir gently over medium heat for 5 minutes, or until lightly browned.

Add the undrained tomatoes and vegetable stock to the pan. Stir and bring to the boil. Reduce the heat to low, cover the pan and cook for 10 minutes, or until the vegetables are tender. Add the basil and pasta and stir until mixed through.

NOTE: Cut the eggplant just before using, as it turns brown when exposed to the air.

Green Curry with Sweet Potato and Eggplant

❧ SERVES 4–6

❧ PREPARATION TIME: 15 MINUTES

❧ COOKING TIME: 25 MINUTES

1 eggplant (aubergine)

1 tablespoon vegetable oil

1 onion, chopped

1–2 tablespoons green curry paste
    (see Note)

375 ml (13 fl oz/1½ cups) coconut milk

250 ml (9 fl oz/1 cup) vegetable stock

6 kaffir lime leaves

1 orange sweet potato, cut into cubes

2 teaspoons grated palm sugar (jaggery)
    or soft brown sugar

2 tablespoons lime juice

2 teaspoons lime zest

coriander (cilantro) leaves, to garnish

kaffir lime leaves, extra,
    to garnish (optional)

steamed rice, to serve

Chop the onion. Quarter and slice the eggplant. Heat the oil in a large wok. Add the onion and green curry paste and cook, stirring, over medium heat for 3 minutes. Add the eggplant and cook for a further 4–5 minutes, or until softened. Pour in the coconut milk and vegetable stock, bring to the boil. Reduce the heat and simmer for 5 minutes. Add the kaffir lime leaves and sweet potato and cook, stirring occasionally, for 10 minutes, or until the eggplant and sweet potato are very tender.

Mix in the palm sugar, lime juice and lime zest until well combined with the vegetables. Season to taste with salt. Garnish with some coriander leaves and extra kaffir lime leaves if desired. Serve with steamed rice.

NOTE: Make sure you read the label and choose a green curry paste without shrimp paste.

Hungarian Casserole

※ SERVES 4–6
※ PREPARATION TIME: 30 MINUTES
※ COOKING TIME: 30 MINUTES

1 red capsicum (pepper)
1 green capsicum (pepper)
1 tablespoon olive oil
30 g (1 oz) butter
1 onion, chopped
4 large potatoes, cut into chunks
440 g (15½ oz) tinned chopped tomatoes
250 ml (9 fl oz/1 cup) vegetable stock
2 teaspoons caraway seeds
2 teaspoons paprika

CRISPY CROUTONS
4 slices white bread
250 ml (9 fl oz/1 cup) vegetable oil

Cut the red and green capsicums in half, remove the seeds and membrane and roughly chop. Heat the oil and butter in a large heavy-based frying pan and cook the potato over medium heat, turning regularly, until crisp on the edges.

Add the onion and red and green capsicum and cook for 5 minutes. Add the tomatoes with their juice, vegetable stock, caraway seeds and paprika. Season to taste. Simmer, uncovered, for 10 minutes or until the potatoes are tender.

Meanwhile, to make the croutons, remove the crusts from the bread and cut the bread into small cubes. Heat the oil in a frying pan over medium heat. Cook the bread, turning often, for 2 minutes or until golden brown and crisp. Drain on paper towel. Serve the croutons with the casserole.

Tofu and Snow Pea Stir-Fry

※ SERVES 4
※ PREPARATION TIME: 10 MINUTES
※ COOKING TIME: 15 MINUTES

600 g (1 lb 5 oz) firm tofu, drained
60 ml (2 fl oz/¼ cup) peanut oil
2 teaspoons sambal oelek or chilli paste
    (see Notes)
2 garlic cloves, finely chopped
300 g (10½ oz) snow peas (mangetout),
    trimmed
400 g (14 oz) fresh Asian mushrooms
    (such as shiitake or oyster), sliced
60 ml (2 fl oz/¼ cup) kecap manis
    (see Notes)

Cut the tofu into 2 cm (¾ inch) cubes. Heat a wok over high heat, add 2 tablespoons of the peanut oil and swirl to coat the base and side of the wok. Add the tofu in two batches and stir-fry each batch for 2–3 minutes, or until lightly browned on all sides, then transfer to a plate. Heat the remaining oil in the wok, add the sambal oelek, garlic, snow peas, mushrooms and 1 tablespoon water and stir-fry for 1–2 minutes, or until the vegetables are almost cooked but still crunchy. Return the tofu to the wok, add the kecap manis and stir-fry for 1 minute, or until heated through. Serve immediately with steamed rice.

NOTES: Sambal oelek is a Southeast Asian chilli paste.
  Kecap manis is an Indonesian sweet soy sauce. If you are unable to find it, use soy sauce sweetened with a little soft brown sugar.

Hungarian Casserole

Spinach and Ricotta Cannelloni

❀ SERVES 6
❀ PREPARATION TIME: 1 HOUR
❀ COOKING TIME: 1 HOUR 15 MINUTES

375 g (13 oz) fresh lasagne sheets
2 tablespoons olive oil
1 large onion, finely chopped
1–2 garlic cloves, crushed
1 kg (2 lb 4 oz) English spinach, finely
    chopped
650 g (1 lb 7 oz) ricotta cheese, beaten
2 eggs, beaten
¼ teaspoon freshly grated nutmeg

TOMATO SAUCE
1 tablespoon olive oil
1 onion, chopped
2 garlic cloves, finely chopped
500 g (1 lb 2 oz) very ripe tomatoes,
    chopped
2 tablespoons tomato paste (concentrated
    purée)
1 teaspoon soft brown sugar
150 g (5½ oz/1 cup) grated mozzarella
    cheese

Cut the lasagne sheets into 15 even-sized pieces and trim lengthways so that they will fit neatly into a deep-sided, rectangular ovenproof dish. Bring a large saucepan of water to a rapid boil and cook 1–2 lasagne sheets at a time until just softened, or about 2 minutes. Remove the sheets carefully with a wide strainer or sieve and lay out flat on a clean, damp tea towel (dish towel). Return the water to the boil and repeat the process with the remaining pasta sheets.

Heat the oil in a heavy-based frying pan. Cook the onion and garlic until golden, stirring regularly. Add the washed spinach, cook for 2 minutes, cover with a tight-fitting lid and steam for 5 minutes. Drain, removing as much liquid as possible. The spinach must be quite dry or the pasta will be soggy. Combine the spinach with the ricotta, eggs and nutmeg and season to taste. Mix well and set aside.

To make the tomato sauce, heat the oil in a frying pan and cook the onion and garlic for 10 minutes over low heat, stirring occasionally. Add the tomato including the juice, the tomato paste, sugar, 125 ml (4 fl oz/½ cup) water and season. Bring the sauce to the boil, reduce the heat and simmer for 10 minutes. If a smoother sauce is preferred, purée in a food processor until the desired consistency is reached.

Preheat the oven to 180°C (350°F/Gas 4). Lightly brush the ovenproof dish with melted butter or oil. Spread about one-third of the tomato sauce over the base of the dish. Working with one piece of lasagne at a time, spoon 2½ tablespoons of the spinach mixture down the centre of the sheet, leaving a border at each end. Roll up and lay, seam side down, in the dish. Repeat with the remaining pasta and filling. Spoon the remaining tomato sauce over the cannelloni and scatter the mozzarella over the top.

Bake for 30–35 minutes, or until golden brown and bubbling. Set aside for 10 minutes before serving. Garnish with fresh herb sprigs if desired.

Tofu in Black Bean Sauce

❀ SERVES 4
❀ PREPARATION TIME: 20 MINUTES
❀ COOKING TIME: 15 MINUTES

1 red capsicum (pepper)
450 g (1 lb) firm tofu
300 g (10½ oz) baby bok choy
    (pak choy)
55 g (2 oz/¼ cup) black beans, rinsed and
    drained
4 spring onions (scallions)
80 ml (2½ fl oz/⅓ cup) vegetable stock
2 teaspoons cornflour (cornstarch)
2 teaspoons Chinese rice wine
1 teaspoon sesame oil
1 tablespoon soy sauce
2 tablespoons peanut oil
2 garlic cloves, very finely chopped
2 teaspoons finely chopped fresh ginger
steamed rice, to serve

Cut the red capsicum in half, remove the seeds and membrane and cut into 2 cm (¾ inch) chunks. Cut the tofu into 2 cm (¾ inch) cubes and chop the baby bok choy, crossways, into 2 cm (¾ inch) pieces. Finely chop the black beans and slice the spring onions, diagonally, including some green.

Combine the vegetable stock, cornflour, Chinese rice wine, sesame oil, soy sauce, ½ teaspoon salt and some freshly ground black pepper.

Heat a wok over medium heat, add the peanut oil and swirl to coat the base and side. Add the tofu and stir-fry in two batches for 3 minutes each batch, or until lightly browned. Remove with a slotted spoon and drain on paper towel. Discard any bits of tofu stuck to the wok or floating in the oil.

Add the garlic and ginger and stir-fry for 30 seconds, then add the black beans and spring onion and stir-fry for 30 seconds. Add the capsicum and stir-fry for 1 minute. Add the bok choy and stir-fry for 2 minutes. Return the tofu to the wok and stir gently. Pour in the sauce and stir gently for 2–3 minutes, or until the sauce has thickened slightly. Serve immediately with steamed rice.

index

Published in 2009 by Murdoch Books Pty Limited

Murdoch Books Australia
Pier 8/9
23 Hickson Road
Millers Point NSW 2000
Phone: +61 (0) 2 8220 2000
Fax: +61 (0) 2 8220 2558
www.murdochbooks.com.au

Murdoch Books UK Limited
Erico House, 6th Floor
93–99 Upper Richmond Road
Putney, London SW15 2TG
Phone: +44 (0) 20 8785 5995
Fax: +44 (0) 20 8785 5985
www.murdochbooks.co.uk

Chief Executive: Juliet Rogers
Publishing Director: Kay Scarlett

Design concept: Heather Menzies
Design layout: Joanna Byrne and Wendy Inkster
Photographer: Jared Fowler
Stylist: Cherise Koch
Production: Alexandra Gonzalez

National Library of Australia Cataloguing-in-Publication Data
Title: Mains
ISBN: 9781741963489 (pbk.).
Series: Kitchen library: Notes: Includes index. Subjects: Dinners and dining. Cookery
Dewey number: 642.4

Colour separation by Splitting Image
Printed by Imago in 2009. PRINTED IN MALAYSIA.

IMPORTANT: Those who might be at risk from the effects of salmonella poisoning (the elderly, pregnant women, young children and those suffering from immune deficiency diseases) should consult their doctor with any concerns about eating raw eggs.

OVEN GUIDE: You may find cooking times vary depending on the oven you are using. For fan-forced ovens, as a general rule, set the oven temperature to 20°C (35°F) lower than indicated in the recipe.